THE EXODUS

E.E.CLEVELAND

REVIEW AND HERALD PUBLISHING ASSOCIATION
Washington, DC 20039-0555
Hagerstown, MD 21740

Copyright © 1986 by
Review and Herald Publishing Association

This book was
Designed by Richard Steadham
Cover art by Lou Skidmore
Type set: 11/12 Benguiat Book Roman

PRINTED IN U.S.A.

Library of Congress Cataloging in Publication Data
Cleveland, E. E. (Edward Earl), 1921-
  The exodus.

  Bibliography: p.
  1. Afro-Americans—Civil rights. 2. Slavery—United
States. 3. United States—Race relations. 4. Christian
life—1960-   . 5. Afro-Americans—Religion.
6. Cleveland, E. E. (Edward Earl), 1921-
I. Title.
E185.61.C626   1986   973'.0496   85-19638
ISBN 0-8280-0299-1

Contents

River of Hope

Waves break against the pier,
debris floats lazily on its silky surface,

But farther out the flow quickens,
things are clearer there.

This is our hope, our River of Hope!

E. E. Cleveland

Introduction

For Negroes the journey to freedom was an unending succession of river crossings. Beautiful yet elusive, liberty seemed to recede with each new advance. Yet the slaves pressed on in their quest and greeted each new day with the expectancy of hope. Freedom denied feeds those curiosities that mother faith. And those who have faith learn to believe despite the absence of evidence and to hope even in the face of contrary evidence.

The slaves' belief that God is just and therefore against oppression weighed heavily in favor of freedom to come. After all, when the Israelites lived in Egypt, God had moved to emancipate them by sending Moses to accomplish His purpose. And so the songs of the slave era reflected those hopes. The slave-preachers' sermons mirrored those dreams. And when the chains of servitude seemed unbreakable, the blacks sang, "Go down, Moses, way down in Egypt land, tell ole Pharaoh to let my people go." Against the gray sky of hopelessness, the slaves unfurled the banner of their faith in the deliverance yet to come.

There are those who think that the Scriptures do not condemn slavery. What a slander on the Word! Did not Isaiah speak about letting "the oppressed go free" and breaking "every yoke" (Isaiah 58:6)? Did not the apostle Paul return a runaway slave to his master with the counsel "Receive him for ever; not now as a servant, but above a servant, a brother beloved . . . both in the flesh, and in the Lord" (Philemon 15, 16)? Emancipation is a divine idea, and slavery is an institution of devils.

Blacks were brought to these shores against their will. For more than two hundred years they worked—without pay—and were at last set free with no land, no job, no home. Segregated, ostracized, and threatened with expulsion, the newly freed slaves knew that between them and freedom stood at least one more river!

A black boy traced circular nothings on the parched red clay.

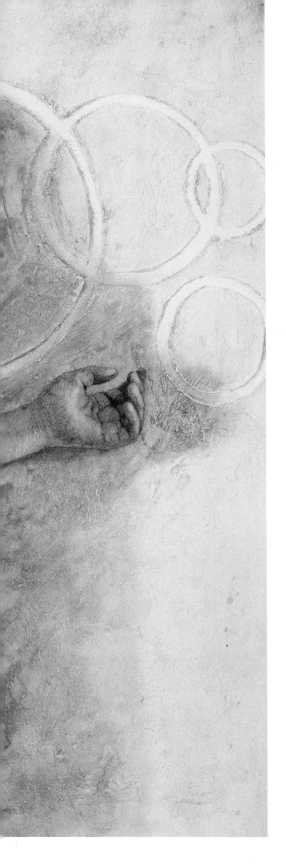

No Stranger Now

The hot summer sun beat down that day in Tennessee. A black boy traced circular nothings on the parched red clay. An angry fly dived repeatedly, stinging its youthful target and altering the broken symmetry of his aimless art.

Thoughts that trouble young teenage minds troubled his. For the moment he was a student of Bonaparte, sweeping in conquest across Europe with the brilliant general. Suddenly, as young minds do, the youth switched channels and was charmed by the oratory of Franklin Roosevelt. "Which will I be?" he asked himself. "A dashing general, leading victorious armies in conquest, or President of the United States, influencing legislation for the uplift of the poor, charming all with my persuasive rhetoric?"

Suddenly the sting of a chigger brought him back to earth. "I can be neither," he scolded himself. "My blood is red, but my skin is black. How far can I really go?"

An invisible line, he knew, adjustable according to the leniency of the bus driver, or lack of it, separated the white section of the bus from the black. Thick walls separated the races in bus and train stations, and the trains provided separate cars. Many blacks bought large automobiles because they were the only motel accommodations available. On countless nights blacks would drive groggily into motel driveways with their "vacancy" signs blinking invitingly, only to be told by an embarrassed clerk, or one with a hard face and hate-filled eyes, "Sorry, I'm full!" This happened both above and below the Mason-Dixon line. When hungry, the "fortunate" black was fed through side doors or back alleys. But no food at all was the rule. Those too proud for this treatment went hungry.

Our old men were "boys," eternally making meaningful the question "How many roads must a man walk down before a man is a man?" Then there were the fears of a people turned in on themselves, and with their fears the attendant violence born of self-hatred. The caged lion, unable to break out, turns upon his own. So has it been historically. To a lesser degree, so is it today.

The black boy scratched the ground thoughtfully with his stick. Everywhere he looked, the skies looked leaden. Blacks earned 30 cents to the white man's dollar. No Negro could enter the white man's baseball leagues. Even if they wanted to watch the game, there was a remote section of the park designated for blacks. The movie industry portrayed the black man as a happy-go-lucky clown or a symbol of subservience. Only by grinning when he wasn't tickled and scratching when he didn't itch could he be labeled a "good boy." Adding to the humiliation was the sure knowledge that many educated community leaders were "bowing the knee" in private to secure certain advantages for blacks.

But there were always men who refused to bow, and these were the architects of the "New Negro." The Fred Douglasses, the Thurgood Marshalls, the Walter Whites, the Martin Luther King, Jrs., and the John Lewises were the vanguard of the new breed. How was our young black Tennessean to know that in a few short years black men and cooperative white men would so alter the course of American history that no level of life or government could deny a man access solely because of his blackness? And how could he imagine that as of this writing the legal battle would be virtually won, and the struggle for implementation well begun?

But only begun, for not all the problems are solved. Indeed, the ones remaining are very real. An estimated 8 to 10 million blacks have not shared even the minimum "American dream." The nation may well direct its best energies to this problem with hast—or see the dream become a nightmare!

That little Tennessee boy is now a man, and he is the author of this book. He has lived to see the leaden skies turn blue, reflecting the clear sparkle of the sunlight. He has thrilled to see the black breakthrough in politics, religion, sports, arts, sciences, and all other areas of American life. And he has lived to see his America acknowledge her

sin of denying recognition of the place of the Negro in exploring and building this country, as well as demeaning his sophisticated African beginnings. Even this knowledge gap no longer exists. There is a new self-respect among black people that can but strengthen the nation.

I have seen the black man rise from the lowlands of ostracism to the very threshold of total acceptance. Will white America go the final mile? Can black restraint await the decision? On the answer to the question the fate of the nation rests. If we have the character to do this, then we well may see on earth "the true community of man." And a wounded people may yet have their pain bathed with the salve of total brotherhood. And in the joy of their restoration they will sing:

"Lord, I ain't no stranger now.
   I've been introduced to the
      Father and the Son,
   And I ain't no stranger now!"

The Africa That Was

"The Dark Continent" was in its earlier history the center of culture for civilized men. North, Central, and South Africa have had their "day in the sun." In the region of the Nile Valley may be found the very earliest signs of culture. The Egyptians were a race whose physical composition flowed from three sources. "The peoples from the eastern Mediterranean world had begun to yield to the temptation to migrate to Egypt. . . . From the east came the Semitic nomads . . . and from the south came the black and brown tribes of Ethiopia."—John H. Franklin, *From Slavery to Freedom*, p. 1.

A fusion of peoples occurred, as is natural in such instances, and therefore a variety of appearances. "The art pieces that have been recovered by archaeologists show a great variety in the appearance of Egyptians, ranging from the Mediterranean type with features usually associated with Caucasians to the distinctly Negroid type with fleshy lips, broad noses, and woolly hair."—*Ibid.*, p. 4. Five centuries before Christ, Herodotus described the Egyptians as being black with woolly hair. Homer also called them black. Count Volney, Napoleon's historian, agrees with Herodotus.

Most probably the Egyptians exhibited a wide variation in appearance, reflecting the three-fold intermixture of peoples. Of the variety of races and their contributions, Franklin says, "Doubtless they contributed heavily, but the constant infiltration of Negroid peoples from the south and the domination by Negroes of the country's political life in its later stages of development, cannot be lightly regarded." Ra Naheci was the first black ruler of Egypt.

Nofretari, wife of Ahmose I, was cofounder of Egypt's Eighteenth Dynasty. She was black and "of great beauty, strong personality, and remarkable administrative ability." By the first thousand years before Christ, blacks dominated the political life of Egypt. Piankhi,

Shabaka, and Taharka were Pharaohs of real stature. They were Ethiopians. Blacks from Nubia helped construct the pyramids and sphinxes, marvels of ancient art and engineering. There was no cultural lag under these leaders. Under Shabaka the temple of Ptah was restored and "buildings were constructed at Tanis, Memphis, and Thebes."—*Ibid.*, p. 9.

The historical record for West and Northeast Africa is replete with matter pertaining to early life in these areas. When the Arabs entered, they found a civilization thousands of years old. Major existing kingdoms were Ghana, Melle, Songhay, and several lesser states. Existing ruins deep in the heart of Africa indicate a high degree of culture in certain areas. The Zimbabwe ruins are a prime example. At Timbuktu there was a university to which scholars came from many parts of the world for study. Other schools were located at Walata and Gao. Ruins formerly ascribed to "outside influences" are now given their proper significance. Now they are attributed to black African origin. Iron was being smelted and tools fashioned while Europe still used crude stone tools.

Certainly the achievements of black men outside of Africa belie the doctrine of racial inferiority. Aesop, Alexander, Dumas, Pushkin, and others have clearly demonstrated Negro capacity in a competitive world. Thus a continent slandered by biased anthropologists, its positive side obscured by historians, now stands revealed for what it was—a land where a branch of the sons of Ham made their place in the sun but later

declined in influence, wealth, and power, succumbing at last to European domination and influence.

Today a few areas in Africa are still occupied by foreign powers. But most of black Africa is free. The spirit of "Uhuru" has swept the continent from Kenya to Ghana, and from the Congo to Malawi. Basking in the sunlight of historical recognition, sons of Africa everywhere may freely sing:

"Lord, I ain't no stranger now."

15

Hope Unborn

Traffic in human flesh is not a recent invention. Ancient nations warred against their enemies, knowing that should they lose they would become slaves to their conquerors. Egypt enslaved the Hebrews for several centuries. Babylon, Medo-Persia, Greece, and Rome have their tales to tell; and none of them are pretty. The Romans enslaved the Greeks and in turn were conquered culturally by them. It is said that the decay of Rome may be laid at the door of her Greek slaves.

With the break up of the Roman Empire, the fragmented states began a power struggle that has not ended as of this day. Besides enslaving thousands conquered in battle, European nations carved up a prostrate Africa into scores of "spheres of influence." The English, French, Italians, Germans, Portuguese, and Dutch made portions of this vast, rich continent their private domains. The riches of Africa poured into Europe, making it the truly affluent area of the world. Britain's colonial empire was so vast that she boasted that the sun never set on it.

Subjected colonial peoples had little power to make decisions on their own. Brutality was the rule in some colonies. In some territories beatings were common, and the people had no court in which to protest the colonial will. While in many instances the foreign power brought medical help, education, and some industrialization, it failed to recognize one of the most fundamental needs of man—passion for human freedom. This flame burns alike in the bosom of black men and white, hence the often bloody upheavals of our own times and the emergence of self-governing African states.

I have traveled in Africa four times in recent years, visiting ten states, and have been deeply impressed with the work of the church. In the early days of colonial expansion, the political governments interested themselves chiefly in the exploitation of the continent's material wealth. The church, however, concentrated on the uplift of the people. Churches established the first elementary schools and colleges. Churches founded the first hospitals. The state, prodded by the church, began to assist on these levels in later years.

Even more important, it was the Christian idea of the fatherhood of God and brotherhood of man that planted the seed of freedom and human dignity in the African heart. Wherever genuine Christianity goes, it brings these results. Europe aroused from her deep sleep only after the coming of Christianity. Much of Asia has had a similar experience.

Christianity did much to help the people of Africa. An outpatient clinic at Mwami Adventist Hospital, Chipata, Zambia. KENNETH MITTLEIDER

Most of the present political leaders of Africa have had some training in Christian schools. Also, the much-maligned missionary has done a splendid job teaching hygiene, moral ethics, dietetics, and child care on a person-to-person basis. Some have imparted other skills such as home construction, farming, budgeting, and secretarial science. The blunders of a few self-styled "messiahs" must not obscure the record of the unselfish many.

But the cruelest aspect of the foreign intervention was the traffic in human flesh, which we call slavery.

By the time the European became interested in the slave trade, the Arabs had already established themselves in this lucrative business. They would convert an African chief to Islam and through bribery secure his tribesmen as slaves. Thus they secured African women for their harems and African men for work. (See Franklin, *From Slavery to Freedom,* p. 43.) If, however, the slave converted to Islam, the Arabs treated him as a brother and he could secure his freedom.

France, Holland, Spain, and Portugal were the foremost European countries to engage in the slave trade, but others followed. The slavers almost stripped some areas of the continent of Africa of the flower of her manhood and womanhood, for they took the strongest and healthiest. By the year 1460, Portugal shipped eight hundred slaves per year to its own shores. With the discovery of the New World the traffic greatly increased. By the year 1540, slaves were shipped to the West Indies at the rate of ten thousand per year.

The slavers kept their captives at slave stations pending the arrival of the ships. The slaves were chained together while marching to these stations, and on board ship. "There was hardly standing, lying, or sitting room. Chained together by twos, hands and feet, the slaves had no room in which to move about and no freedom to exercise their bodies even the slightest."— *Ibid.,* p. 56. This was over three thousand miles of ocean. With no allowance for toilet facilities, one can imagine the horror and stench of "the middle passage." Smallpox and other diseases took their toll. Thousands died at sea from disease, suicide, and bleak dismay.

An estimated 3 percent of blacks captured died on African soil in forced marches to the sea. Nearly 33 percent died during passage at sea. Another 13 percent died during the "break-in" period—from three to four years spent "bending" the captive to perpetual slavery in theory and practice.

This attrition of the people was like driving a dagger into Africa's heart, for the slave trader demanded "the healthiest, the largest, the youngest, the ablest, and the most cultured." They numbered in millions. The black man was on his way to the New World, where for years he would be a pilgrim and a stranger. That other blacks had preceded these as explorers of the New World would be quickly forgotten in the rush for riches. It would be a long time before, on these shores, the black man would sing, "Lord, I ain't no stranger now."

A Thousand Midnights

"War and slavery were almost universal twin relics of barbarism," Dumond has written. "Let us," he continues, "examine the lack of legal personality, of positive rights, on the part of the slave. The law denied him the right to think, to receive religious instruction, or to worship in a church of his own choice; the right to move about beyond the limits of his master's property; the right to marriage, parental authority, and protection of home. The right to own, accumulate, inherit, or bequeath property. . . . The slave enjoyed no security in his own person. The law gave the slave owner the power of punishment even to the extent of killing the slave. Society gave to any person apprehending a slave abroad the right to chastise him; it punished the slave severely, sometimes with death, for striking a white person even in self-defence: it (the law) defined the rape of the female slave as trespass on the owner's property; and it ignored forced concubinage and prostitution. The slave could be punished in anger, for vengeance, and out of pure sadism. No one ever knew why, or cared, or paid attention to what went on even at the public whipping posts. . . . They were expected to breed like animals, remain ignorant and unprotected by the law, yet to obey the law. They ran away and were hunted down by bloodhounds, wantonly shot, publicly whipped, and mutilated by branding."—Dumond, *Antislavery*, pp. 14, 15.

The name for all of this is slavery. But there is no word that can encompass the experience. Who can measure the pain of a mother's heart as men tear her child from her bosom and carry it away? Or of a brother, father, or husband sold to a different plantation owner? What comfort is it to a husband to realize that his wife is the object of the slave master's lust and there is no protection? What is it like to be driven to the fields before sunrise and marched home after sunset with nothing but backbreaking toil in between? With no doctors to care for sickness, the slave must find the right herb or die. Only if prostrate is he released from duty. Permitted only the coarsest diet, he lived and died knowing nothing of the dainties that adorned the master's table. No one will ever know how many bodies were concealed in the marshy swamps or swiftly flowing rivers. Sons and daughters of former masters may sing with nostalgia, "Way down upon the Swanee River," but they will get little accompaniment from the sons of former slaves.

Of the contrast between American slavery and Moslem slavery we read, "Truth and justice demand from me the confession that the Christian slaves among the barbarians of Africa are treated with more humanity than African slaves among Christians of civilized America."—W. O. Blake, *History of Slavery in Northern Africa*, p. 79. From Theodore D. Weld's *American Slavery as It Is* I quote, "They were often stripped naked, their backs and limbs cut with knives, bruised and mangled by hundreds of blows with a paddle, . . . shot down like beasts, torn to pieces by dogs, . . . their ears are often cut off, eyes knocked out, bones broken, maimed, mutilated, and burned to death over slow fires. And this was intended by law to be perpetual."

Many armed insurrections occurred against white oppression. Some familiar names of the revolution are Denmark Vessey, David Walker, and Nat Turner. A poet has rightly described American slavery as "blacker than a thousand midnights." The miracle of black survival is the riddle of our time. And yet there is an explanation.

A shaft of light from heaven pierced the midnight of black sorrow. A few masters taught their slaves to read the Bible. Some religious gatherings were permitted. The black preacher between frequent groans and mutterings would inject gems of Scripture bright with hope and promise of better days to dreams of a downtrodden people and encouraged them to hope against hope for the breaking of the day.

The slave also learned the power of prayer. To him the "earthly skies were brass." He therefore clung to the belief that Jehovah, the Deliverer of Israel, would someday set him free. The ability of the black man to pray with passion was born in those dark years.

"Stony the road we've trod,
Bitter the chastening rod,
Felt in the day when hope unborn had died."
—James Weldon Johnson
"Negro National Hymn."
And then, there were his songs!
"My Lord delivered Daniel,
I know He'll deliver poor me."
Faced with perpetual servitude, a helpless minority could only sing,
"Over my head, I see trouble in the air.
There must be a God somewhere!"
The black man was to see his faith rewarded. There is indeed "a God somewhere." And happy is the man who understands this.

O Freedom

In whatever bosom the human heart beats, its rhythmic message is freedom, freedom. Nowhere is the human incapacity of man to dominate his fellowman more clearly demonstrated than in the American experience with slavery. In a nation dedicated to freedom, with liberty and justice for all, existed the foulest blot ever to stain the conscience of mankind—human bondage. Some Bible expositors who identify the lamblike beast of Revelation 13 with the United States interpret its gentle qualities as its Constitution and Bill of Rights, and the speaking "as a dragon" as the voice of the oppressive system of slavery.

But a nation that promised so much could never survive denying so much to so many. In the language of a great statesman: "No nation can long endure half slave, half free." And it is still true that "a house divided against itself cannot stand." Either America would guarantee the full privileges of citizenship to all or she would eventually be helpless to deliver freedom to any. For the day would come when neither the conscience of the majority nor the patience of the minority could bear the burden of guilt. Thomas Jefferson, in 1806, congratulated the Congress that it at last could "withdraw the citizens of the United States from all further participation in those violations of human rights which have been so long continued on the unoffending inhabitants of Africa, and which the morality, the reputation, and the best interest of our country have long been eager to proscribe."

The voice of Christianity was the decisive factor in mounting the offensive against slavery. As early as 1671 George Fox, founder of the Quakers, spoke out against the slave trade. From then on a growing sentiment pressured the British government to act. David Rice, a Presbyterian, coauthored with David Barrow in 1807 a treatise on slavery, appealing to reason in their condemnation of it. John Rankin wrote in the Ripley, Ohio, *Castiga-*

tor, "I consider involuntary slavery a never failing fountain of the grossest immorality, and one of the deepest sources of human misery. It hangs like the mantle of night over our republic, and shrouds its rising glories. I sincerely pity the man who tinges his hand in the unhallowed thing that is fraught with the tears, and sweat, and groans, and blood of hapless millions of innocent and unoffending people."—Dumond, *Antislavery.* Joining Rankin were Dickey, Gilliland, Lockhard, and Crothers, all Presbyterian ministers. James Duncan, a minister from Indiana, lifted his voice against this nefarious trade. He declared slavery contrary to the Constitution of the United States, and likewise condemned all State laws supporting it.

Methodist camp meetings also became antislavery rallying points. On August 16, 1818, Pastor Jacob Gruber preached so forcefully against the trade that he was indicted by a grand jury for sedition and put on trial. Numerous societies for the freedom of slaves were organized, most of them church sponsored. Also church-sponsored schools took up the cudgel.

"The great revival gave the antislavery movement an unprecedented number of devoted apostles. They had the writings of Woolman, Rush, Hopkins, Cooper, Rice, Branagan, Barrow, Duncan, Clarkson, and Wilberforce. They needed all this and more to beat down and destroy the doctrine of racial inequality, enshrined in slavery, and upheld by the courts . . . and the political parties."—*Ibid.* And what of William L. Garrison, the

Quakers, and that band of intellectual preachers, Tappan, Bourne, Leavett, Goodell, and Weld, not to mention Greeley, Parker, and Frederick Douglass?

Ellen G. White, an internationally known Seventh-day-Adventist lecturer, aimed her pen at the slave trade: "In this land of light a system is cherished which allows one portion of the human family to enslave another portion, degrading millions of human beings to the level of the brute creation. The equal of this sin is not to be found in heathen lands."—*Testimonies,* vol. 1, p. 259.

John Byington and Joseph Bates were also ardent Adventist antislavery advocates. Today the church is criticized for having upheld the slave system. While this is true of much of religion, it is just the opposite with others. History is clear: To Christianity we must give credit for the leveling of the temple of human bondage to the dust. The voice of God, through the church, paralyzed the slave trade and turned it back.

The Civil War wrote the final chapter of the story of human bondage. Until the slaves were freed, peace was impossible. When they were emancipated, things moved rapidly. In all fairness, it should be pointed out that thirty-eight thousand blacks died in that war. More than two hundred thousand fought in its most famous battles—Vicksburg, Petersburg, Richmond, and Shiloh. They fought in Appomattox Courthouse, April 9, 1865. The blood of blacks and whites mingled on a common battlefield.

A mysterious force was at work in

it all, which students of the Bible recognize as the finger of God in human events. Egypt was plagued until she freed the Hebrew slaves. Indeed, a part of the program of God is to "let the oppressed go free." Similarly, this nation was plagued with war that would not end until the slaves were freed.

While the aims of the North were yet unclear, she could not carry the day. Lincoln in the early stages was vague in his expressions on abolition. His purpose, he stated, was to "save the Union." The freedom of blacks was a secondary issue. The Southern forces, outnumbered and underarmed, won victory after victory. The Northern giant moved as if in a trance. Could it be that the hand of God was over it all, safeguarding the interests of the slave? The evidence indicates that this is so. Abolitionists thundered and lobbied. The slaves prayed and

fought. Northern politicians agonized and vacillated. Crisis hung heavy in the air. The silver cord of the nation's life had nearly snapped.

The nation fixed its eyes on one man: Lincoln. Would the nation live or die? The God of heaven, moved by the agony of the oppressed, had ordered a modern Moses to "let My people go!" Came the night January 1, 1863. Lincoln had entertained more than three hundred guests and shaken their hands at the time of departure. And now he sat at his desk deep in contemplation. He lifted his pen over the document that would go down in history as the Emancipation Proclamation. His hand trembled so violently that he hesitated. Then with resolution he affixed his signature—Abraham Lincoln.

The slave exulted.

"O freedom—O freedom—O freedom over me,
And before I'd be a slave—I'd be dead and in my grave
and go home to my Lord and be free!"

Church bells pealed the joyous news. The burdened conscience of the nation found new relief. The angel of peace began his journey to the earth. Northern armies moved with a new sense of resolution. Victory followed victory. Lee was cornered in his native Virginia. Sherman marched to the sea. Two men, Grant and Lee, faced each other in a house.

It was all over. America had by a violent operation arrested the progress of a terminal malignancy. She was now free to seek her place in the sun. The slave would have his "jubilee."

Where
Shall I Go?

Emancipation? Not the end, but the beginning of a long, slow trek from the Egypt of slavery to the promised land of full citizenship in this Republic.

After the high exhilaration of emancipation, there dawned the slow realization that in order to free all slaves Congress must enact additional legislation. Congress reconvened in 1865, determined to control reconstruction. Thaddeus Stevens, Republican from Pennsylvania, guided the Congress through the passage of the Fourteenth Amendment of the Constitution. The South rejected this and began the enactment of segregation laws that plagued this nation for one hundred years. Congress proposed the establishment of a Freedmen's Bureau to help the newly freed slave find employment and readjustment. President Andrew Johnson vetoed voting rights bills, and an angered Congress overrode the veto. The black man now had the Thirteenth and Fourteenth Amendments, the civil rights act of April 9, 1866, and the Freedmen's Bureau on his side. How now could America fail to keep its promise to the black man? The answer is not easy.

In the South, after the war, Southern politicians seized the initiative as state legislators passed the black codes, a set of repressive laws specifically designed to keep the black man in an inferior position. These laws were multiplied and copied throughout the Southern States, so that overt segregation or ostracism, with the force of law, replaced slavery. Thus the black man found himself barred from the ballot box and from most public facilities, shunted to the back of public conveyances, given the worst jobs or none at all, paid with low pay or no pay, given a poor education or none at all, housed in poor housing or none, and that in segregated districts. Unpaved roads, poor toilet facilities or none, and infrequent garbage collection added to the black man's peril. Add to this the Ku Klux Klan, a terror

American blacks endured the indignity of segregated public facilities. UPI/BETTMANN NEWSPHOTOS

organization that did its work by night, and we have a fair picture of the bleak conditions that faced the black man in those days. The very motivation behind the segregation laws was unholy. Representative Barry, of Virginia, addressed his colleagues concerning the Negro thus: "Gentlemen, we have succeeded in shutting out all light from him. It remains for us to render him incapable of perceiving light, and our task is done."

Having failed in perpetuating slavery, men worked busily to make impregnable the walls of segregation. Neither could succeed. The prayer of the black man had been heard in heaven. He was on his way.

"Another agency that offered both spiritual and material relief during reconstruction was the Negro church."—Franklin, *From Slavery to Freedom,* p. 308. Consigned to the galleries or otherwise ostracized by white Christians, blacks began to form their own churches, and in them they found the fellowship lacking in former relationships. And in the South, subtle pressures were applied to preserve the dual pattern of worship so that interracial gatherings were permissible only if separate seating arrangements were maintained. As late as 1942 some cities were still trying to enforce this. In my own public meetings I never arranged for separate seating. This cost me much in terms of white attendance, but nothing can compensate for the feeling that one is doing right.

Politically the South was divided into military jurisdiction during Reconstruction. The Reconstruction Act gave the Negro the ballot, and he used it. Negroes were elected to the State legislatures and drew up in their States' progressive constitutions, including provisions for public school systems and voting reforms. Proof of the wisdom of

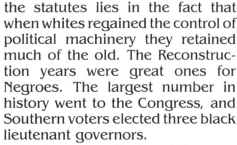

the statutes lies in the fact that when whites regained the control of political machinery they retained much of the old. The Reconstruction years were great ones for Negroes. The largest number in history went to the Congress, and Southern voters elected three black lieutenant governors.

As long as Federal troops remained in the South, black men had a chance at liberty and respectability. It was Rutherford B. Hayes who, as President of the United States, made a deal with the South and withdrew Federal troops, leaving Negroes at the mercy of vengeful whites. In the ensuing years more than five thousand blacks were victims of lynching. The grisly history of these years makes sensitive men shed tears. Racial laws were passed with vengeance, some so outlandishly slanted and degrading as to render obedience to them a violation of the Law of God. Blacks, North or South, knew no security. Blacks and whites battled in the streets. The New York riots were among the most notorious. Blacks were excluded from juries, and given long sentences and heavy fines by the courts.

But the churches began to move in the field of education. They established colleges all over the South for the education of black youth: Clark, Morehouse, St. Augustine's, Shaw, Oakwood, Johnson C. Smith, Dillard, and others. These schools still graduate more blacks than any others.

Again it was the church that moved to the relief of the oppressed while politicians debated the place of the black man in American society. The church

with its teaching of the fatherhood of God and the brotherhood of man prepared the blacks for the days ahead. Of equal value was the character-building program that provides the best motivation for life and service.

Then two giants came on the scene with two separate philosophies. They were Booker T. Washington and W.E.B. Du Bois. Each achieved considerable success. Like Martin Luther King, Jr., of the sixties, these men dominated their era. King's philosophy was to embrace much of both men's ideas. Let us first consider Booker T. Washington.

His philosophy rested on two cornerstones: " '(1) In all things that are purely social we can be as separate as the five fingers, yet one as the hand in all things essential to mutual progress; and, (2) To those of my race who depend upon bettering their condition in a foreign land or who underestimate the importance of cultivating friendly relations with the Southern white man . . . I would say, "Cast down your bucket where you are—cast it down in making friends in every manly way with the people of all races by whom we are surrounded. Cast it down in agriculture, in mechanics, in commerce, in domestic service, and in the professions." ' "—*Ibid.*, p. 391. He encouraged intelligent management of farms, ownership of land, and good manners. He urged, " 'I would set no limits to the attainments in letters or in statesmanship, but I believe the surest way to reach those ends is by laying the foundation in the little things of life, that lie immediately at one's door.' "—*Ibid.*, p. 392.

W.E.B. Du Bois, a young Fisk graduate with a Doctor of Philosophy degree, opposed Washington's view. He said, " 'If we make money the object of man-training, we shall develop money-makers, but not necessarily men. If we make technical skill the object of education, we may possess artisans, but not mature men. Men we shall have only as we make manhood the object of the work of the schools.' "—*Ibid.*, p. 393. Du Bois conceded that Booker T. Washington was the acknowledged leader of his race but maintained that this was by choice of the whites, not the blacks.

In subsequent years the Du Bois theory won out, and Negroes embarked on a "white collar" educational training. Thousands poured through the gates of the nation's best-known educational institutions. But in the early years few were admitted to jobs for which they were trained. Some college graduates became street sweepers. The black man learned that not even training could overcome the color bar. Education, culture, and refinement did little to guarantee financial security, social acceptance, or housing in the neighborhood of one's choice. In short, the black man found himself a stranger in his own country. Having turned his back on Booker T. Washington's industrial-education theory, he lacked land and training in the skills of industry; and, though educated, he did not enjoy the full privileges of citizenship. The plaintive wail of the Negro spiritual found new significance: "Where shall I go but to the Lord?"

For his survival the black man would need, not one course of action, but three: (1) The Washington philosophy of education in productive skills; (2) the Du Bois theory of training in the arts, sciences, and humanities; and (3) a thorough grounding in the Christian religion and its character-building virtues. The Du Bois theory would have prepared, and did indeed prepare, thousands for "white collar" jobs necessary for the degree of assimilation that was then future, and for educational work in the black community. But a people without capital is a dependent people. A landless people is a generation of consumers. The Booker T. Washington theory would have provided the black man with a larger, more broadly based middle class, which in turn would have provided capital for more jobs, thus reducing unemployment and underemployment. And how we need this now!

In the long frustrating years since emancipation, the church has played an increasing role in the black man's life. It became the center of the social acceptance denied him in everyday life. The Scriptures provided motivation necessary for survival in this society and for citizenship in the celestial one to come. The greatest danger to any race or nation is that in moments of disappointment or elation it may in anger or exultation forget God. The acceptance or refusal of rulers and people to acknowledge the God of heaven as king of all the earth has been the key to the rise and fall of empires.

"I the Lord thy God am a jealous God," Jehovah thunders. There can be no ignoring or evasion of Him. People simply refuse to grasp this lesson. In the language of the song we ask, "When will we ever learn?" Will the black man repeat this madness? Will he, either through burning anger or prosperous affluence, turn from the God who emancipated him? His rapid rise has startled the civilized world. No people in history with comparable obstacles has risen so far so fast. Will the heady elixir of success turn his reason? Or will he be sobered by the knowledge that "righteousness exalteth a nation: but sin is a reproach to any people"?

After emancipation the black man moved toward his wilderness. The law, courts, schools, and financial institutions favored the white man. To overcome this injustice seemed indeed a formidable task. But the blacks undertook it.

Black inventors showed the way. Jan E. Matzeliger, John Parlser, Elijah McCoy, and Granville T. Woods were but a few. These men were responsible for many inventions from the shoe lasting machine to devices having to do with steam boilers and automatic brakes. Negroes began to enter the business world. Black men founded the Bay Shore Hotel, Hanyston, Virginia; Capitol Trust Company, Jacksonville, Florida; Southern Stove Holloware and Foundry, Chattanooga, Tennessee; the Madam Walker Beauty establishment; the North Carolina Mutual Insurance Company, of Durham, North Carolina; and many others. But these were not enough. Booker's theory was slow to catch on, and the black man entered the wilderness.

The Wilderness

The tight noose of segregation slipped perceptibly as the black man emerged from the Reconstruction era. As America entered the twentieth century, she found her segregation laws in conflict with her conscience. The black man was to test that conscience until it hurt. Americans would later realize that in a democracy such as this all or none are free.

In 1914 Europe was convulsed in a great war, and three years later American troops crossed the Atlantic to battle the Germans. The kaiser had taken on the world. Black troops fought in the American Army, but largely as a group. In the main, they were led by white officers. They were, however, liberally used as service battalions. There was an early relunctance to arm black men in large numbers, but as the war intensified, blacks assumed an increasing role in the actual fighting.

When it was over, the black man returned to America expecting to find things better than before. But he found little relief. The Klan continued to ride, and rigid laws continued to repress. The stock market crashed in 1929, plunging the nation into the great depression. Blacks were the first to lose their jobs as the crisis deepened. I remember as a boy seeing long lines of men in front of government dispensaries receiving hard bread and thin soup for their families. Times were hard for most Americans, but black Americans suffered most.

"Happy days are here again;
The skies above are clear again;
Let us sing a song of cheer again.
Happy days are here again!"

Then Mussolini moved into Ethiopia and raped that helpless state, reducing it to an Italian satellite. Haile Selassie, emperor of Ethiopia, appealed in vain to an apathetic world for support and relief. His words fell on deaf ears. He was pathetically prophetic when he predicted that the world would regret its decision to sacrifice his nation.

31

Soon Hitler was on the move into the Sudetenland and eastward to Poland. Alarmed, the world sprang into action. Ethiopia tested the willingness of the West to fight. Neville Chamberlain confirmed their reluctance. German military lightning struck Poland. The Poles fought violently but were simply overwhelmed by the mightiest war machine in the world. I visited Poland in 1959. They had rebuilt the cities and only a few visible scars remained. Despite indescribable suffering, the Polish spirit never broke.

England entered the war. Germany attacked Russia. The Japanese bombed Pearl Harbor. America was again at war. The Air Force could boast of its 99th Pursuit Squadron, made up of blacks, which served in the Mediterranean. The 92d Army Division, also black, received five hundred forty-two Bronze Star decorations, eighty-two Silver Stars, twelve Legion of Merit awards, and more.

Then President Harry Truman integrated the Armed Forces. Black GIs fought with their white brothers on all major battlefronts. In Europe, across the Mediterranean, and in the South Pacific the blood of blacks and whites mingled to form a crimson trail around the world.

But on the mind of every black soldier were questions: What will things be like when the war ends? Will the sacrifices made by black men in war change things for them in their neighborhoods back home? Slowly, all too slowly, the war in the Pacific and Europe came to a close. And the trickle of soldiers homeward became a flow. But things had not greatly changed

back home. The best jobs were still for nonblacks; so were the best schools, homes, neighborhoods, and service establishments. A first-class black soldier was still a second-class citizen. Nikita Khrushchev could stay in hotels where American blacks could not, and skin color was the sole difference. Then came the sixties.

The Martin Luther King, Jr., era had its beginning in 1955 with the organization of the Montgomery Improvement Association. Dr. King was catapulted into the national limelight when his organization came to the assistance of Mrs. Rosa Parks, who resisted the Jim Crow laws in bus seating in Montgomery, Alabama. The struggle over the segregated bus issue was long and tense. A nervous nation watched transfixed as the drama unfolded. Mass meetings were held to dramatize the issue. "We shall overcome" became the theme song of the dispossessed. Ralph David Abernathy emerged as the number two man in the movement. The court struck down the segregation laws. The nation breathed easier, but not for long.

Freedom rides into Alabama and Mississippi were making the headlines. Beatings and bus burnings were the order of the day. James Farmer of CORE distinguished himself during these years as he led wave after wave of blacks and whites against the bastion of segregation. Fred Shuttleworth, a local Birmingham minister, started an independent campaign against segregated bus and train stations. He was jailed and otherwise mistreated until joined by King and Abernathy. Pictures of the ensuing struggle sickened the conscience of the nation. Police dogs, fire hoses, and billy clubs hastened the collapse of segregation laws in all Alabama. The universities of Alabama and Mississippi desegregated.

In North Carolina a group of young students sat down at segregated lunch counters and asserted the right of the hungry to eat there. This direct confrontation precipitated similar actions all over the nation at swimming pools, restaurants, motels, and other public places. The names of John Lewis and Stokely Carmichael as leaders of the Student Nonviolent Coordinating Committee captured headlines.

These young people penetrated the Deep South and instructed black people in voter registration procedures. They opened freedom schools to advance the cause. Thousands of whites were involved in these movements directly, and others supported the movement with their money. Without these white allies, progress would have been impossible.

Then there was Malcolm X, the tough-talking Muslim leader who militantly asserted the equality of blacks with whites. In all fairness, it should be pointed out that he taught that blacks should defend themselves against attack. He did not teach violence as an aggressive tactic, only as self-protection. Malcolm X greatly influenced the present crop of young people and their stance.

With all these forces at work, progress in race relations was rapid, clear, visible. Under Presidents Kennedy and Johnson, hopes soared that solutions could and would be found.

Solutions! All human solutions are but patchworks if they do not reach the human spirit. Apart from Christ there is no healing. Nineteen hundred years ago the Son of God invaded human history with solutions that solve and answers that satisfy. But the world had not yet had its fill of mad Caesars, and they lynched Him on a tree. The world would yet have to face its Napoleons and its Hitlers.

When man turns his back on God, there remains only the yawning abyss of human sorrow. There is no answer without Christ! Can we who know so much be ignorant of this? Then for this foolishness we will pay with our lives! But need we?

There is a better way. "Behold the Man!" "He was wounded for our trangressions, he was bruised for our iniquities" (Isaiah 53:5). Our sins and all of their attendant problems were with Him on the tree. But He did not leave the solution there. By the shedding of His blood, Jesus Christ offers His life of peace to warlike man.

Be it forever remembered that this was no ordinary man at Golgotha's brow. Jesus Christ was God in the flesh. Man therefore has no problems that can baffle Him. The race and the nation are indebted to Him for life, liberty, and the pursuit of happiness. It is not the genius of man that has forged this nation or effected the black man's freedom. But by the will of Jehovah it has all come to pass. Only God knows the way through the wilderness, and all we need to do is follow.

Martin Luther King, Jr.: "I have a dream."

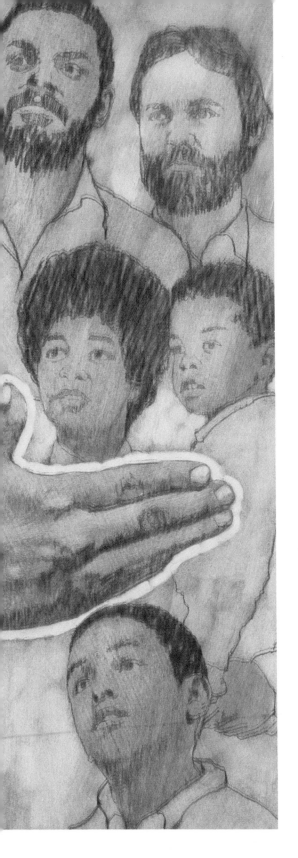

The Mountaintop

Every movement has its moment in the sun, its finest hour. The march on Washington August 28, 1963, was that moment of brightest promise for the civil rights movement in America. An estimated 500,000 people of all races gathered in the capital to voice their faith in the American dream. The inspiration of it all moved the conscience of the nation. At last we were on our way, or so it seemed. From the moment the first bus disgorged its passenger on the Mall till the thrilling intonement of "I have a dream" echoed in the summer air, it was in truth the nation's golden moment. It was our mountaintop!

I was sitting in a darkened room in Dar es Salaam, East Africa, with my ear glued to a transistor, through which this saga of man was borne to us over the ocean waves. It was a demonstration without violence, the largest in our history. No nation in history had succeeded in providing so much for so many. At this one moment there was the fleeting feeling that "maybe we could pull it off." Congressmen, labor leaders, businessmen mingled—men of all walks of life. Bare feet dangled in the cooling waters of the reflecting pool as speaker followed speaker. Roy Wilkins, Walter Reuther, John Lewis, Whitney Young, Adam Powell, and Philip Randolph brought into focus the significance of the day with painfully pointed rhetoric.

The last speaker of the day was Martin Luther King, Jr. He had hardly begun his message when it was apparent that this was to be his day. He spoke the thoughts of millions when he proclaimed his dream of an America free for all Americans. The world heard his voice that day and thrilled to his message. The little man dared hope again, and "feeble knees" were strengthened. Justice would "run down as waters, and righteousness as a mighty stream." The rough places (and there are plenty of them) would be made plain and the crooked places straight. The mountains would be leveled and the valleys exalted.

Strong men wept. Black babies pressed to their mothers' bosoms would someday receive the benediction which that day foreshadowed. The day ended in a surge of emotion as the setting sun framed in its golden glow the mighty climax:

"Free at last, free at last;

Thank God Almighty, I'm free at last."

In the gathering gloom the crowds dispersed. As quietly as they came they returned to unchanged neighborhoods to await and work for the fulfillment of the promise.

The road to the mountaintop had been long and hard. There were Little Rock and the courageous Daisy Bates and her husband. There was James Meredith at Oxford, Mississippi. There was Medgar Evers, ambushed in the driveway of his home for his courageous, humane approach to civil rights. But it was Thurgood Marshall who changed the law, and for this he has earned the respect of the nation and the world. Black people must never allow their children to forget him!

Relief for the poor had begun with Franklin Roosevelt. Harry Truman went further and integrated the armed forces of the nation. Then came the Kennedys—John F. and Bobby, brothers who seemed to understand. The Kennedys grasped the meaning of human freedom and shared this spirit with the nation. Assassins' bullets aborted their missions. Then came Lyndon Johnson, a white man and a Southerner by birth. Under his administration the nation at last desegregated itself legally. He identified with the poor and sought to move the nation to do the same.

But the dream of human equality received several jolting setbacks. The brutal murders of the Kennedys benumbed the nation. And the assassination of Dr. Martin Luther King, Jr.,—the focal point of much of the visible change that is now evident—tested the survival of the nation. King's death plunged the advocates of peaceful change into a state of dark despondency. The voice of the peacemaker had been silenced. James Baldwin's book *The Fire Next Time* seemed

more than prophetic as city after city went up in flames. Thousands of people gave vent to their wrath in a rage of burning and looting. A mad act provoked an angry answer.

America has not quite recovered her balance since. A sense of fear, suspicion, and foreboding has gripped the nation. Youthful anger rends proud campuses. The old retire behind their prejudices. Some politicians live to exploit it all. As frightened whites strive to retain the status quo, black militance is on the rise. Few dare predict just where it all will lead. But clearly we are in a state of internal crisis. The idealisms of the sixties are not being voiced. There is a dangerous polarization at work in our land. Thousands are arming themselves for some racial conflict that must never happen! Hatemongers are having a field day inciting suspicion and fear. Heady, threatening talk from black and white compounds the frustration. The world beholds in wonder a nation whose technology can place men on the moon, but whose races have not learned to share this planet in peace.

Actually, two years before the death of King conservative whites began to assert themselves, slowing the pace of integration. And, with this new resistance, black militance rose rapidly. King felt keenly the slowdown of the integration pace. Chicago and other Northern cities resisted the efforts of minorities to penetrate the de facto segregation status.

Dr. King and SCLC turned to the plight of the poor. Dr. King championed the cause of the poor man. With his staff he planned the poor people's march on Washington.

There was a strike of the sanitation workers in Memphis, Tennessee. Dr. King led a march that ended in violence. He determined to prove that nonviolence was possible and that the voice of the poor could still be heard in the land. In the last mass rally that he was to address he forecast his own death. "I have been to the mountaintop," he said. He predicted that we would reach the promised land. He doubted that he would cross with us. But, he thundered, "Mine eyes have seen the glory of the coming of the Lord."

The coming of the Lord—blessed thought! That will be the day when every man will be free—when there will be no rich, no poor, no sickness, no death. Perhaps men have attempted too much without Him and trusted too much in social methods and the so-called innate goodness of man, rather than in the power of God as it was revealed in a sin-pardoning Saviour. Perhaps we have not really lived the slogan on our coins, "In God we trust." It just could be that the coming of the Lord is the only event that will bring men life, liberty, and the happiness that they have so long pursued in vain.

Black Is Beautiful

I sat in an audience of two thousand, listening to an eloquent plea for racial harmony and tolerance. With captivating sincerity the lady speaker voiced her hopes for the America that could and can be. She decried the hate that rends this nation to its vitals. She pleaded for this country to spare itself the agony of further division.

Who was she? She was Mrs. Medgar Evers. On a still, hot night in Mississippi a shot had rung out, and her husband had fallen a martyr to the cause for which he lived—human freedom. She held his head in her arms as he lay bleeding to death. Hers was the most famous teardrop in America, for *Life* magazine featured on its cover the sad, beautiful face of this young widow, a single tear and its trail visible on that grief-stricken countenance. Hers was the most difficult task of all—that of comforting her little children. How indeed do you explain a thing like this to fresh young minds? In a sense, hers was the burden shared by thousands of her black sisters over the centuries from slavery to this day. Black mothers and fathers have had the staggering responsibility of explaining segregation, slavery, and ostracism. They have not done a good job. Who could? To explain it, like explaining sin, is to justify it. This has been a part of the "black man's burden."

There this young widow stood, having forgiven the nation for the hate that produced the killer of her husband, pleading for reason in an atmosphere of passion, for patience instead of precipitous action. And I whispered, "Black is beautiful."

The city was Memphis, Tennessee. Marching thousands chanted freedom songs as they moved toward city center. At their head strode the slain leader's widow, Mrs. Coretta King. With steady step and tilted chin she marched. What memories must have crowded her mind as the marchers swayed with the rhythm of their music and prancing feet. The atmosphere

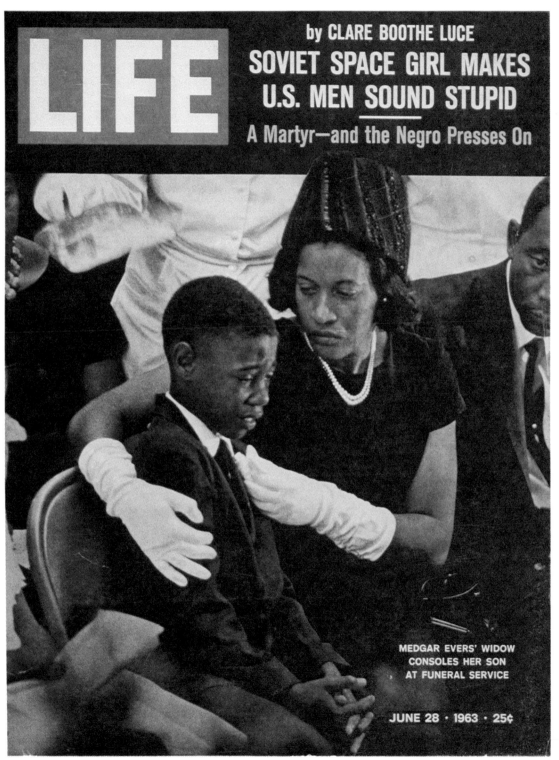

by CLARE BOOTHE LUCE

LIFE

SOVIET SPACE GIRL MAKES U.S. MEN SOUND STUPID

A Martyr—and the Negro Presses On

MEDGAR EVERS' WIDOW
CONSOLES HER SON
AT FUNERAL SERVICE

JUNE 28 · 1963 · 25¢

Mrs. Medgar Evers at her slain husband's funeral. JOHN LOENGARD, LIFE MAGAZINE © 1963 TIME INC.

seemed to crackle with tension. Was another sniper, his brain crazed with hate, peering intently from another window in search of another victim? Could the nation's nerves stand another killing? Hardly, but something inside her said that her husband's march against injustice must be completed. So there she was, completing a mission.

She marched with memories. Chicago, Birmingham, Washington, and Selma all combined in this last great march. It was an attempt to save the nation's soul. She spoke that day, the resonance of her voice strangely reminiscent of that of her departed husband. She too had forgiven the nation whose atmosphere had spawned a James Earl Ray. And I said, "Black is beautiful."

Some years before, a man had stood strangely erect though stooped, the deafening applause of the Congress of the United States ringing in his ears. It had been a long journey from a slave's cabin to this exalted lectern. He had been traded for a racehorse to one Moses Carver. Mrs. Carver, a kindly woman, taught him to read and write. As was the custom in those days, the slave was given the surname of his slave master. He took the name George Washington Carver.

The applause echoed and re-echoed through those historic halls, so long accustomed to the sound of political oratory. But this was different. Before them stood a black scientist. This was history. They had given him a brief few minutes to speak. But these men had been so charmed by his astuteness and wisdom that they had lost sight of time. This man, who had saved the economy of the South, gave the glory to the "Great Creator." He taught Southern farmers to grow something on their land besides cotton. He persuaded them to grow peanuts, and then he discovered more than three hundred uses for them. He discovered the language of the plants and was often in conversation with growing things. With few he shared his secrets but he made his discoveries available to all. He refused untold wealth to dedicate his life and service to his people. It is amazing that from a man so shy that he ran when my wife sought his autograph came a wisdom that still defies human explanation.

His speech finished, his shoulders sagged visibly as he strode quickly through the Senate chamber to the door. These were for him unfamiliar surroundings. He was more at home in his cluttered laboratory, or in the Alabama forest conversing with nature's creatures. He had forgiven the nation the fact that as a boy he was traded for a horse. He had saved the economy of a region that had defamed black daughters and lynched black sons, and would do so for years ahead. He had risen above it all and had become an acknowledged giant of his time, and all time. As I view him now in historical perspective, I whisper, "Black is beautiful."

One of the more serious legacies of slavery was self-hatred. In a variety of ways the slave was taught to despise himself. He was taught that his hair and skin color were the result of a divine curse. Robbed of his history, he knew nothing of his past. One hundred years after emancipation, textbooks in American schools still ignored the contribution of black Americans to the building of America, picturing Africa as a perpetual "dark continent." This systematic dehumanization took its toll, and it is reflected in the crime statistics of the nation. Rob a man of his sense of worth and you destroy his better self. In slavery and for years thereafter this nation sowed the wind, and now it reaps the whirlwind.

In an age of great enlightenment such as this, it is inevitable that light should break through and that the truth about African history should be known.

For years Carter G. Woodson and J. A. Rogers were voices crying in the wilderness, asserting the historical dignity of black people. Tribute is also due thousands of black teachers who taught young blacks the available facts at the risk of losing their jobs. Then came Mordecai H. Johnson and John Hope Franklin, who pulled the historical records together and closed the knowledge gap. The cultural contributions of blacks to the world are now known, and religious denominations are also changing attitudes. Jesus was neither white nor black, and who knows the color of the angels? As for the City of God, "all nations, kindreds, tongues, and peoples" will fellowship in per-

fect harmony there.

With the rapid filling of the knowledge gap, the black community feels a new sense of dignity. There was a song in our history,

"I'm coming, I'm coming,

For my head is bending low;

I hear those gentle voices calling,

'Old black Joe!' "

But in the black community these words are no longer heard. The song has been paraphrased:

"I'm coming, I'm coming,

And my head ain't bending low.

I'm talking loud and walking proud——

I'm America's new black Joe!"

Beginning in 1962 the change in the mood of black people about themselves became evident. The freedom rides, the Montgomery bus boycott, and the student sit-ins began to have their effects. It was as if a people long asleep had awakened to a new sense of self-worth. We now accept our hair, skin color, and other physical features as evidences of God's blessing, not a curse. We see and appreciate the peculiar beauty that is ours. Now we feel a basic and essential love of ourselves and each other that slavery had prevented or destroyed. As a people we have "come alive."

White America need not be threatened by all of this. It is as though an organ of the body, long dormant, is now healed and functioning. The rest of the body must adjust to this new situation and benefit by it. Did anyone really believe that after he educated a man and permitted him to worship God he would remain a slave? Quoth the raven, "Nevermore."

But blacks must not overvalue blackness as whites have their whiteness, or we will only compound the present madness. We will, if we fail here, merely substitute black wickedness for white. Then historians will sadly shake their heads and write, "We've seen it all before." There is but one guarantee against destructive pride for black and white, and that is a personal relationship with Christ. Men who fight God must fight each other. The very basis of all morality is love for God and man. A people without love are people without life. They are given over to purposeless vengeance.

Have we come this far only to "get even" for past injustices? At most this policy can but destroy the nation for us all. For some, this may be enough. Only madmen, black or white, could find satisfaction in standing Tarzanlike on the ruins of the nation's cities thumping their chests in glee, boasting that they have taken vengeance one of the other. Yes, we can ruin it for each other, but is there time to build on the ruins? If so, what shall we build?

On a college campus recently a young man challenged me, "Give me one reason why we should not burn it down!"

My answer was simple: "First, you have no right to destroy what you did not help build. What have you put into the foundation of this nation? Your black fathers helped build this country with their blood, sweat, tears, and wisdom. And you burn it down? Is that the best you have to offer? Second, things have opened up so beautifully in the past fifteen years that this country deserves better than this. Let it stand, and change it for the better!"

Next Time

Cain, eldest son of Adam, killed Abel. Thus violence was born on this planet, and it has grown to be an earth-threatening monster whose symbol is the mushroom cloud. Violence is increasing, perhaps because of years of conditioning; and thus its final acceptance comes as a normal part of life. It now threatens to become a permanent way of life.

Not long ago men were genuinely shocked by murder, war, and its attendant mutilations. But no more. Two global wars, with men in all lands trained to kill, have taken their toll of human sensitivity. The mass media, with their vivid portrayals of crime in awesome detail, have further conditioned us to the routineness of violence. Headlines no longer shock; spilled blood no longer horrifies. The world seems violence-hardened. And this, for all of us, is dangerous.

The instruments of violence are many, and some are sophisticated, ranging from knives to nuclear missiles. The basis of all of this is

fear. Each individual and nation must "protect itself." New weapons must be added because the other fellow increases his arms. But where will it all end? Can men store such arms permanently without use? And where will they dump these things left unused? In the sea to contaminate plant and fish? Or will they bury them and defile the soil?

The basis of violence is the false concept that might makes right. International diplomacy has coined the phrase "negotiate from strength." But does not history teach us that the mighty today are the weaklings tomorrow, and that advantage gained from brute strength is temporary at best?

History seems to support this proposition. Napoleon, Charlemagne, Kaiser Wilhelm, Hitler. If a dictator rules a year, each day seems an eternity. But in the long view nothing really permanent is established by force. Napoleon Bonaparte acknowledged this. In exile, near the end of his life, he

recognized that the kingdom of Jesus, based on love, had outlasted all others.

The deadening of conscience toward violence is a gradual thing. But we knew it had happened to us when we could listen to reports from battlefields with as little concern as we listened to weather reports. And when a public official could urge that a country be bombed into the "stone age," our change was completed. Some of us saw it coming. The Bible long ago predicted it. The uncovering of the Nazi mass graves did little to help. But the most important single factor in the deadening of the human conscience was the creation of the bomb, a monster that defies all description in its capacity to destroy. Single blasts incinerated Hiroshima and Nagasaki. The cities just disappeared. The nuclear fallout altered the genes of survivors.

We feel a sense of hopelessness from the mere existence of this weapon. It appalls us; there seems no escape. Added is the spectacle of orbiting space stations from which an enemy may hurl these lethal eggs to earth at will. How can the human spirit survive, knowing of the brutality of these grisly instruments of death? Man has become his own executioner, bent on self-destruction in the name of self-defense, not knowing when or where—only how. Our children hear about megatons and missiles. They are conceived in fatalism and fed on the opiate of frustration. Is there any wonder that such sacred occasions as commencement exercises are satirized to the point of comedy, and beatniks make a shambles of the ritual?

You, reader, must be able to identify the sickness, or you and the nation will turn to clubs, guns, and tanks to subdue what you will not take the time and patience to resolve.

Or perhaps you, too, have lost hope and are content to play out your plastic part until the end. We cannot go on supporting false theories and perpetuating hollow values that veil human hypocrisy. Something can be done about this world and the quality of life on it. Yes, the Bible says there will be wars and rumors of war, but it also says, "Blessed are the peacemakers." And the same Bible that predicts rampant disease, earthquake, and tidal wave also commands the relief of the oppressed.

There is no religion in merely reciting the dire predictions of the Holy Scriptures and, having done so, withdrawing to one's tower of isolation to watch the evil come to pass. There is nothing in the events themselves that is self-perpetuating. It is the sinful perversity of man that has affected all nature, weakening the power of nature's laws to control her. Jesus Christ has provided in Himself at Calvary the peace and power to imitate Him, the original peacemaker.

But how can a man live meaningfully in the shadow of the tomb? The answer is so simple that it is difficult. A doctor knows that death is inevitable, even his own, yet he lives to die but he gains his joy by cheating death by the practice of his skills one more day, hour, month, or year. Ask any doctor how he functions meaningfully in the face of death, and he will tell you of joy at seeing a given disease arrested and death turned aside. He will speak of human gratitude, the thanks of the healed and the relieved. He will declare life worth living, as it is for all who find life's challenge for them and accept it.

There is much to encourage us: Thousands of Peace Corps workers and Vista Volunteers labor untiringly in unfamiliar surroundings to make life better for those less fortunate. Government is willing to relate itself to the poor in many ways. There is still hope when millions can agonize with three men traveling in space in a crippled spacecraft and sigh with relief at splashdown and recovery. There is still hope when men and women on a highjacked airliner emerge safely from their ordeal to the cheers of thousands. There is hope when we can feel for and help the earthquake victims of Peru and the starving kids in American cities. Yes, there is still hope.

But we must nurture hope. As a mother, bending over her newborn babe, we must feed it. It will bring relief to our hearts, joy to the world, and "sorrow and sighing will flee away." And we shall at least postpone the fulfillment of these prophetic lines of a Negro spiritual:

"God gave Noah the rainbow
    sign.
 It won't be water, but fire
    next time."

The Promised
Land

"Walk together, children; don't
you get weary.
There's a great camp meeting in
the Promised Land.
There'll be a jubilee, O my Lord,
There'll be a jubilee way over on
the old campground."

Soon after the emancipation the
camp meeting, or "association,"
became the occasion for wide-
spread fellowship and rejoicing
among black Americans. Denied
social contact and acceptance
accorded others, the Negro took
refuge in the church. It became the
social center of the black world. The
membership gathered quarterly for
worship and social fellowship.
"Potluck" dinners were served out-
doors under the shade of trees,
heavy with green. The meals were
called potluck because nobody
ever knew what anybody else would
bring until the various dishes were
assembled.

Spirited preaching and exhorta-
tion took place at these one-day
gatherings. Emotional exhibitions,
shouting, and verbal ejaculations
accompanied a "good" sermon—
this is a matter of record. Little
understood, however, are the reasons for such unbridled emotion.
The pressures of day-to-day living
for blacks discouraged free expression. To survive, they had to
repress their feelings and opinions.
Only in church were they free,
feeling none of the inhibitions that
plagued them during the week.
Thus the emotion displayed at the
camp meeting was likened in the
spiritual song to a "jubilee."

This world, however, plagued by
six thousand years of problems
consequent to sin, can never be the
promised land of our dreams.
Human judgment at its best is
subject to grave imbalance. Majority justice is in its nature self-contra-
dictory. Human history rarely records long-continued justice for all
anywhere. The strong have controlled the weak, the poor, and the
few in numbers. There have indeed
been uprisings, and this equation
has been temporarily upset, only to
yield in time or to revert to the law of

human selfishness. And when the conquered replace the conquerors, there occurs little variation in this pattern. From time to time good men rule, and the lot of the weak is improved. Alas, if history is to be trusted, this too shall pass. We may never expect utopia under human supervision.

Nevertheless, utopia will come! But how?

The Bible alone has the answer: "And in the days of these kings shall the God of heaven set up a kingdom, which shall never be destroyed: and the kingdom shall not be left to other people, but it shall break in pieces and consume all these kingdoms, and it shall stand for ever" (Daniel 2:44). The phrase "and the kingdom shall not be left to other people" is significant. People, other than the Lord, have polluted the kingdoms now existent. Man has oppressed man and rendered this planet unfit for human habitation. We must therefore look to God alone for the fullest realization of our utopian dreams. And there is ample evidence that He will not disappoint us. "For, behold, I create new heavens and a new earth: and the former shall not be remembered, nor come into mind. But be ye glad and rejoice for ever in that which I create" (Isaiah 65:17, 18).

For permanent change to come, God will have to intervene personally in human affairs and reestablish His own righteous rule on the earth. And this He has promised to do. "Let not your heart be troubled: ye believe in God, believe also in me. In my Father's house are many mansions: if it were not so, I would have told you. I go to prepare a

place for you. And if I go and prepare a place for you, I will come again, and receive you unto myself; that where I am, there ye may be also" (John 14:1-3).

Christ has promised to come again to this earth. That coming will be catastrophic to the life proud man has built without God. "The earth shall reel to and fro like a drunkard, and shall be removed like a cottage; and the transgression thereof shall be heavy upon it" (Isaiah 24:20). This will mark the end of man's reign on the earth. Ultimately God will indeed set up His own kingdom here. In it, "the eyes of the blind shall be opened, and the ears of the deaf shall be unstopped. Then shall the lame man leap as an hart, and the tongue of the dumb sing: for in the wilderness shall waters break out,

and streams in the desert" (chapter 35:5, 6).

He will banish poverty in His kingdom, and there will be no unemployment, no high rent for poor housing. "And they shall build houses, and inhabit them; and they shall plant vineyards, and eat the fruit of them. They shall not build, and another inhabit; they shall not plant, and another eat: for as the days of a tree are the days of my people, and mine elect shall long enjoy the work of their hands" (chapter 65:21, 22).

There will be no segregation there, for judgment will "run down as waters, and righteousness as a mighty stream" (Amos 5:24). And "every valley shall be exalted, and every mountain and hill shall be made low: and the crooked shall be made straight, and the rough places plain: and the glory of the Lord shall be revealed, and all flesh shall see it together: for the mouth of the Lord hath spoken it" (Isaiah 40:4, 5).

He will abolish death and all cause for sorrow. "And I saw a new heaven and a new earth: for the first heaven and the first earth were passed away; and there was no more sea. . . . And I heard a great voice out of heaven saying, Behold, the tabernacle of God is with men, and he will dwell with them, and they shall be his people, and God himself shall be with them, and be their God. And God shall wipe away all tears from their eyes; and there shall be no more death, neither sorrow, nor crying, neither shall there be any more pain: for the former things are passed away" (Revelation 21: 1-4).

No one will be a stranger there!

Heaven on Earth

The hand of the emancipator Abraham Lincoln trembled violently as he stood ready to sign his preliminary Emancipation Proclamation. The night was September 22, 1862, and this act would go into effect January 1, 1863. When the slave was emancipated, no plan existed for his rehabilitation. Turned loose in a hostile society, he had to make his own way with no advantages. In the South, where most of the slaves dwelt, conditions resembled an economic wasteland. Some whites were so poor that they replaced horses in pulling the plows while others pushed in order to till the soil. Therefore, the former slave master could do little for the newly freed slave, and such hostility existed that there was little that any would do.

However, many former slave masters went into partnership with their slaves, and together they rebuilt their economy. Federal troops imposed an uneasy peace, while blacks in the South enjoyed their first taste of liberty. Ruther-

ford B. Hayes, however, betrayed the black man and withdrew Federal troops from the South, resulting in the segregation laws that persisted there for many years. By then, in both the North and the South, blacks found themselves forced to live in certain specified areas which, due to the population explosion, mushroomed into the large all-black neighborhoods known today as ghettos. For thousands here in the inner city, the values and the goals differ from those found in the suburbs. In many instances, the problem is one of meeting the everyday needs necessary for survival. In the ghetto few people puzzle over investments, and the stock market might well refer to the inhabitants of a cow pasture.

The Emancipation Proclamation left freed blacks to fend for themselves, although the Freedmen's Bureau did much to find jobs for many of them. Neighborhood lines hardened as whites became more affluent and as blacks bought the

Civil Rights marchers arrive at the Lincoln Memorial, August 28, 1963. UPI/BETTMANN
NEWSPHOTOS

houses that the whites had evacuated, even though many of the houses were in an advanced state of decay.

Now affluent blacks are on the run with increased prosperity, and they are buying into the suburbs, leaving the cities to their fate. But the pattern still follows that when blacks move into a neighborhood, even in the suburbs, the whites, in turn, move farther out into suburbia so that, in effect, we have two residential Americas—black and white.

Thus, America set up a dual set of economics so that in 1969 the Negro's average income was 64 cents to the white man's dollar. It evolved a dual system of education, and, because of the neighborhood system, there usually existed a dual system of religious worship, since people normally attend the church nearest them. For years under segregation laws, black people smarted under the insult of having to ride in the back of public transportation vehicles, enter special side doors of restaurants, and sit in what was dubbed the "buzzard's roost"—a section of the balcony of theaters and concert halls that were frequented by whites. They felt especially apprehensive when walking or driving in white areas of the cities. They used "colored" rest rooms, drank "colored" water, and were never allowed to forget for one moment that they were "colored." For this reason the black community today hates the term *colored*.

The favorite term in the Negro community is *Afro-American*. Another popular term is *black*, which seems to be as accepted as *Negro*.

In the ghetto there is also a different view of police protection. Among whites, even little children look affectionately upon the neighborhood officer, who is, indeed, their big brother and has been so traditionally. But the black community fears white officers and in many instances despises them because of their traditional role in the community. Officers today who find themselves misunderstood need only consult the history of law enforcement in the ghetto to understand the reasons; and, unfortunately, these reasons may bear no relationship whatsoever to the individual conduct of an individual white officer who works in the ghetto today. Traditionally, blacks, even when innocent, have run at the sight of an officer. I can remember my childhood fear of police, who could stop you at any point and call you "boy" or "nigger," and you dared not object for fear of having your skull laid open with a billy club or being shot to death on the spot. In times past some law enforcement officers have been known to participate in lynching and cold-blooded murder.

Thus, the average Negro grows up with mixed feelings about the police. It came as no source of security for us to learn that any Negro could be suspected as a lawbreaker no matter how well dressed or respectable he may be and that only by reacting "humbly" could he expect to escape the wrath of the long arm of the law. As a result, such organizations as the Deacons and the Black Panthers have arisen. A kind, considerate, but firm and thoroughly disciplined police force would have eliminated the necessity for either organization.

Now this does not negate the fact that there are now and always have been some splendid police officers who always operated within the bounds of law enforcement propriety, but it is also true that to the average black man an officer's badge has represented the oppressive arm of the segregationist establishment. This is the view from the ghetto.

I might also point out that this suspicion of law enforcement carries through to the courtroom, which, in times past, has given Negroes long sentences for "minor infractions," whereas whites similarly convicted have either been reprimanded or given short sentences. Thus the phrase "respect for law," so common among whites, has another interpretation in the ghetto, namely, "respect for law that respects me." Ghetto dwellers do not blindly accept "law and order," for they clearly and painfully recall the not too distant past when some State legislatures deliberately enacted laws that would demean, degrade, and debase all black people. Many students of history remember the time when the Federal government even sanctioned slavery. Therefore, the phrase in the black community is "law and order with justice."

In all the wars that this country fought, youths from the ghetto have conducted themselves well, but the reader of this book should know their motivation. While whites went into World War I to "make the world safe for democracy," blacks went in for quite a different reason. They felt that by proving themselves good soldiers, they would make America safe for black people back home. In World War II, white Americans went out to "safeguard the free world" against the intrusions of Mussolini and Hitler, but black soldiers had quite a different motive. Many fought like tigers, hoping they would so impress their white counterparts that their own country would change its laws and recognize them as human beings when they came back home.

Only in the most recent past has the mood really changed among black people to where they have begun to sing with a greater degree of fervor, "My country, 'tis of thee, sweet land of liberty." Within these few years, America has changed for the better. To be sure, not fast enough nor far enough, but it has changed. And we are now on the threshold of a momentous opportunity. We are within view of the fulfillment of its promise to all its citizens of "life, liberty, and the pursuit of happiness."

Where will America go from here? At this critical moment, it needs cool tempers, calm speech, and dogged determination to realize the American dream and to extend its privileges to all citizens. Only a Christ-oriented conscience can accomplish this. Only men whose hearts God's unselfish love has captivated can possibly achieve the utopia our Constitution promises. Unless grounded in God's love, our faith will fail us now. All our dreams of an America free from racial bias and discriminatory laws will collapse in a dead heap at our feet unless the miracle of divine grace transforms us, white and black, into genuine "soul brothers." This must, indeed, be more than a political stratagem. It has to be a spiritual commitment, for the whole idea of brotherhood is Heaven-born. God, the great Creator, made us His sons and, therefore, brothers to each other. Were we to show this love, it would transform every ghetto into a little heaven on earth. It would redirect the resources of the nation to the plight of the poor and the needs of the underprivileged in our country. Love would convert hovels into palaces and rat-infested neighborhoods into gardens of beauty.

No Room for Hate

Few know the well-documented facts of the part black men have played in founding and establishing America. Thirty black men accompanied Balboa when he discovered the Pacific Ocean. We know the name of one of them, Nuflo de Olano. When Alvarado went to Quito, he carried two hundred Negroes with him. They also accompanied Pizarro on his Peruvian expedition and carried him to the cathedral after he was murdered. Negroes in the expeditions of Almagro and Valdivia saved their Spanish masters from the Indians. They accompanied Narvaez on his expeditions in 1527 and were with Cabeza de Vaca in the exploration of the southwestern part of the United States.

The celebrated Lewis and Clark Expedition, which left St. Louis in 1804 and headed for the Pacific, carried at least three black men with them. One by the name of York, a giant in size and strength, was good-natured and got along well with the Indians. As a matter of fact, they looked upon him as a god because of his stature and liberally supplied him with their women as they would a god. They regarded him as leader of the expedition when he was only the interpreter. Another Negro, Pompey, also accompanied Lewis and Clark on their dangerous northwest expedition, and a pillar in Montana has been named after him. We could repeat this record again and again in the histories of Georgia, Mississippi, and Louisiana, but let us move rapidly to the defense of freedom and independence in this country.

During the wars with the Indians, Negroes figured prominently. In the pacification program in 1676, a black named Jethro saved the Plymouth Colony from what might have been total massacre. For this great service they rewarded him by setting him at liberty in two years. The record of this deed says, "I do not find anywhere else an adequate acknowledgement. The Englishmen of Plymouth Colony were

Crispus Attucks died in the defense of American liberty. LIBRARY OF CONGRESS

[indebted] to this Negro for saving Taunton from destruction."—*Plymouth Colony Records* (1676), vol. 5, p. 216.

Negroes helped General Wolfe capture Quebec from the French in 1759. They also helped at Fort Duquesne, Pennsylvania, under General Braddock and his successor, General Washington. Braddock, wounded in that fight, gave Bishop, his Negro bodyguard, to Washington. Bishop served George Washington faithfully for the duration of the war. Whenever Washington rode on parade, Bill Lee, a black, rode immediately behind him. On March 5, 1770, Crispus Attucks died in defense of liberty on the Boston Commons. He is listed as the first to die in the Boston Massacre, and the colonies observed Crispus Attucks Day until the day that independence was won. From that time the July 4 celebration has replaced Crispus Attucks Day.

At Fort Griswold, a Negro deftly threw a spear and killed the British commander, Major Montgomery, as he mounted the parapet for a charge. And at Newport, Rhode Island, an African by the name of Prince captured, with his own hand, Major General Prescott, the commander of that colony.

Altogether, in excess of five thousand blacks fought in the Revolutionary War, playing a prominent part in the expulsion of the English from American soil.

One added note. Prior to the battle of New Orleans, Andrew Jackson, on September 21, 1814, appealed to the blacks for help in a last desperate effort at victory. In the second week in December, as the British sailed up the Mississippi with twelve thousand men in sixty ships, the Americans mowed them down as on they came, wave after wave. After losing four thousand men in two weeks, the British finally sailed away.

After the battle, Jackson addressed the Negro troops, "Soldiers, when on the banks of the Mobile, I called you to take up arms, inviting you to partake in the perils and glory of your white fellow-citizens, I expected much from you; for I was not ignorant that you possessed qualities most formidable to an invading enemy. I knew with what fortitude you could endure hunger and thirst, and all the fatigues of a campaign. I knew well how you loved your native country, and that you, as well as ourselves, had to defend what man holds most dear—his parents, wife, children, and property. You have done more than I expected. In addition to the previous qualities I before knew you to possess, I found among you a noble enthusiasm, which leads to the performance of great things.

"Soldiers! The President of the United States shall hear how praiseworthy was your conduct in the hour of danger, and the representatives of the American people will give you the praise your exploits entitle you to. Your General anticipates them in applauding your noble ardor."

Yet not until thirty-six years later, in 1851, was the gallantry of those Negroes who fought at New Orleans publicly remembered in an anniversary parade.

During the Civil War, 200,000 blacks fought, and 38,000 lost their lives fighting for their own personal

freedom.

Two hundred and fifty years of slavery had buttressed the economy of Europe and America, for Europe profited by the slave trade, and America built its economy on the backs of blacks. But only after the abolition of slavery did this nation become the technological giant that it now is. The determined atacks of American whites with blacks gave their enemies no quarter until slavery was banished from the land. When they finally succeeded in removing the curse of slavery, America became, indeed, "the land of the free and the home of the brave"! Prospered of God, it began to grow in influence and power until it stands second to none as a world influence.

But where do we go from here? A troubled nation ponders its future as the eyes of the world focus upon it. The American system of government has made possible the most rapid development of a minority people that world history has ever known. No other minority group has arisen in only one hundred years to the present eminence that American blacks now enjoy, and America has done it, not only with the assistance of some whites but over the violent objections of others and despite the obstacles put in its path. Through it all the black man never lost his love for his country or his determination to achieve the freedoms that others enjoy. The American experiment must succeed, for it is man's last chance to build a nation dedicated to freedom, with liberty and justice for all.

The haters and the bigots, both black and white, must take a backseat in this critical hour of America's history. Men and women dedicated to justice, freedom, equality, human dignity, and brotherly love must speak out now, or we shall one day peer out from between charred branches, twisted skyscrapers, and molten steel, lamenting the land that might have been.

The missing link in the black man's struggle for dignity has now been supplied. History accords him the credit due him for his part in building our nation. And today in the arts, sciences, government, economics, religion, medicine, sports, and all other fields of human endeavor, black men equal and excel others in the performance of their duty. But this story must be told and retold until the facts of history chasten those with superiority attitudes. Those who have been cowed by a lack of knowledge of the glorious past that black men have shared with others may now look up, lift up their heads, and walk with dignity like men.

But there simply must not occur a reverse racism that would lead to the hatred of whites on the part of the blacks. Due to our orientation toward Christianity, we have been taught to love our enemies, to bless them that curse us, and to do good to them that despitefully use us. Without lifting up arms against our brothers and turning this nation into a caldron of racial hatred, we have come this far along the ladder of human progress. We cannot afford to "blow" it now. James Weldon Johnson put it:

"Stony the road we trod,
Bitter the chast'ning rod,
Felt in the days when hope unborn had died;
Yet with a steady beat,
Have not our weary feet
Come to the place for which our fathers sighed?
We have come over a way that with tears has been watered:
We have come, treading our path through the blood of the slaughtered,
Out from the gloomy past,
Till now we stand at last
Where the white gleam of our bright star is cast."

May the Star of Bethlehem light our way and the Man of Calvary soften and subdue our hearts, and may we, with measured step and hearts secure in the knowledge of our own dignity, move into the future, hand in hand with our white brother. It is a curious fact that our interests are so intertwined that default on the part of one would mean the destruction of the other. We've come a long way together, and "black and white together, we shall overcome."

Is There Room
in the Inn?

After 240 years of enforcing slave labor, America responded to its religious leaders and astute statesmen, who pounded its conscience until it erased the foul blot of slavery from every facet of its national life. Few realize that slavery began in the northern part of the United States, but as the industrial revolution came first to the North, slave labor became unprofitable and so crept into the South. The southern part of the United States, then largely an agrarian society, seemed ideally suited for slave labor. Thus slavery flourished in the South, which only reluctantly yielded under the persistent hammering of Generals Ulysses S. Grant and William T. Sherman.

The Thirteenth and Fourteenth Amendments of the Constitution ultimately freed all slaves north and south of the Mason-Dixon line. In addition, the Fourteenth Amendment declared them citizens of the United States and thus entitled them to all its privileges and responsibilities.

The white American was in the majority and found himself facing a dilemma. What should he do with the thousands of recently freed blacks in terms of their social responsibility? Though the Constitution guaranteed no discrimination, legislators hastily framed State laws that would ensure the physical separation of the races and economic and social subjugation of the black man. Thus America's first move in determining the social status of the recently freed Negro physically separated him from the rest of society, guaranteeing that he would never emerge from his "pigeonhole."

Immigration laws were fixed so that only a limited number of Africans could enter this country in any given year, while almost unlimited immigration privileges were granted those from Europe, especially from the northern and central sections of Europe. When these European immigrants entered this country, the government granted them free plots of ground in the

West, lent them money for implements to till the soil, hired farming agents to teach them the art of farm developments, established land-grant colleges for the perfection of this expertise, and paid them thousands of dollars as subsidies to let portions of their land periodically rest from tillage. Contrast this with the treatment of the black man when he received his freedom.

Despite his 240-plus years of free labor, he received no free plot of ground on which to make a new start. Cut off from gainful employment, nobody taught him any of the skills necessary to compete in American society. He was not admitted to the established colleges of the day, and the government sent out no supervisors to

teach him a new way of earning a livelihood. That the race survived at all is a miracle, attributable only to the loving beneficence of an all-wise God.

Gradually religious organizations began moving to the rescue of the black man. The Federal government followed and established a chain of black colleges across the nation, the oldest of which is D.C. Teachers College, established in 1851. Soon in practically all the Southern States colleges were erected for the training of the black man, and he began the long ascent "up from slavery."

The government had still not decided just what place it would assign the black man in the life of the nation, even though the Constitution now declared him a full citizen. Abraham Lincoln toyed with the idea of exporting the black man to Africa, and, indeed, the Federal government did send a limited number of Negroes to Liberia as an experiment in black colonization. Today the republic of Liberia owes its present existence to this experiment. However, the black man, in general, had no enthusiasm whatsoever for exportation because he had lived here from the beginning of this country, fought in all its wars (including the Civil War), participated in the exploration of the West, and had had 240 years of unrequited toil exacted from him. Understandably he felt then, as he does today, that this is his country too.

At long last, the Federal government began to understand this and embarked on a course of "separate but equal" treatment of the Negro, although in practical effects sepa-

rate was never equal. Alongside this program ran another of limited integration, so that the policy of the government toward the Negro could be called neither segregation nor integration but a fusion of the two. Under this plan the great bulk of black people were segregated, but always a few broke through in every field of occupational endeavor, including the Federal government itself. Only recently have the State governments begun reflecting more broadly the different constituent elements of their populations.

Faced with this inconsistency, little wonder that thousands of blacks lost their lives, not knowing which phase of an inconsistent plan applied in a given place at a given time. A black, while traveling along the highway, may have stopped at a service station for gasoline, but he never knew when he could or could not use the restroom facilities of that station, even though he paid his money for the gasoline. Just within the past decade, a returned war veteran was shot in cold blood for having mistakenly assumed what should have been a natural privilege.

Today America still pursues this alternating policy, though there is no Federal or State law that, in theory, segregates a citizen. However, in practice, the dual system still continues. To illustrate: A black man's moving into a neighborhood is followed by flurry of whites getting out, until another neighborhood becomes a part of the "ghetto area."

After years of Federal law to integrate the schools, we have succeeded in integrating only a small percentage of the nation's educational institutions. These "straws in the wind" may indicate that American whites have little will or desire to regard black men as equal citizens under the law and as human beings who make desirable neighbors. The present course of events seems to indicate that in the foreseeable future most blacks will continue to live in predominantly black neighborhoods, while most whites will continue to inhabit the suburbs. A sprinkling of blacks will infiltrate all suburbs, but the bulk of the population will remain physically separate in terms of living quarters. With the present polarization of attitudes, the prospects for totally assimilating, dispersing, and integrating the Negro are dim indeed.

A study of human history offers little hope, for we find no record of a majority completely absorbing a minority while that minority continued its racial identification. Absorption has usually meant either the disappearance of the minority or its subjugation. The American experiment, then, though bold and laudable, when viewed in the light of history, cannot possibly succeed in the "melting-pot" aspects of the program. The simple fact is that at no time, in any place—on American soil or elsewhere—has a community of men lived and worked together without regard to racial identity.

Although the American Constitution promises this, history has condemned it to failure. It seems that in the future our nation must set a course toward fraternity, coexistence, identity of interests, and integration where it can and does work; but where it doesn't, it must make life livable and equitable in the large ghetto areas that will still dot our nation. From the large black communities must come representatives who will defend in the halls of government the upgrading of life in the ghetto community. Increasingly, blacks must be encouraged to man their own business enterprises. Streets must be paved, housing updated, and adequate salaries paid the workers from the ghetto for services rendered.

If America follows such a policy, it may yet go forward to fulfill its dream of being a land vast in beauty and unlimited in opportunity, where every man is guaranteed the privilege of "life, liberty, and the pursuit of happiness."

History affords only one example of a minority surviving a majority— the Jew, and his formula is simple. At those local areas where life is most meaningful, Jews work together and cooperate for the common good, sharing with a less fortunate brother until he can get on his own feet. Then he, in turn, extends the service. At those levels of government above and beyond the Jewish community, Jews manage to enter them all, thus turning the resources of goverment for the betterment of the Jewish community. For the immediate future, this course appears best for the American black man. So that the Federal government may best spend its energies in this direction, we should now embark upon a policy of "unity through diversity," envisioning a nation morally strong, sensibly secure, and worthy of its position as a world leader.

Why do some prosper while others have such a difficult time?

Fix Me, Jesus, Fix Me

The Negro spiritual that says "We are way down here in Sorrow's Valley, come see about me" reflects the dilemma that has puzzled Christians throughout the centuries. Just why do the wicked apparently prosper while the righteous have such a difficult time? Is it a fact that this is so? Or, does it only appear so?

When the world was in its most perfect condition, and that, of course, was in the Garden of Eden, where Adam and Eve enjoyed a perfect environment, a test determined their fitness to enjoy the privileges that were then theirs. "And the woman said unto the serpent, We may eat of the fruit of the trees of the garden: but of the fruit of the tree which is in the midst of the garden, God hath said, ye shall not eat of it, neither shall ye touch it, lest ye die" (Genesis 3:2, 3).

Adam and Eve failed the test. Sin invaded this perfect environment, and all nature lost its original beauty and harmony. Now man has more than a tree to contend with, and when it seems that all the sacrifices he makes come to naught and all the good that he does means nothing, his problems often puzzle him.

David puzzled about this in the seventy-third psalm: "For I was envious at the foolish, when I saw the prosperity of the wicked. For there are no bands in their death: but their strength is firm. They are not in trouble as other men; neither are they plagued like other men. Therefore pride compasseth them about as a chain; violence covereth them as a garment. Their eyes stand out with fatness: they have more than heart could wish. They are corrupt, and speak wickedly concerning oppression: they speak loftily. They set their mouth against the heavens, and their tongue walketh through the earth. . . . Behold, these are the ungodly, who prosper in the world; they increase in riches" (verses 3-12).

This is the Christian's dilemma. Having done his best, he often finds himself in trouble right up to his neck, and he looks on the wicked and sees them prospering. Money in the bank, automobiles to ride in, and comfortable homes are attractive assets, to say the least. But often the wicked have them and the righteous do not. So David began to pity himself. "Verily I have cleansed my heart in vain, and washed my hands in innocency. For all the day long have I been plagued, and chastened every morning" (verses 13, 14). But a change took place in this man, for when he needed to understand something, he knew where to go. "I went into the sanctuary of God; then understood I their end" (verse 17).

When you are discouraged and burdened down, that is the worst time in the world to stay away from church. Go to the sanctuary where God is, where His Word is read. There you will find understanding. There light will penetrate the darkness of your mind and bring again the sunshine of God's joy. Your heart will again hear the singing of the warbler and the gentle rustle of the leaf. Once again your heart will know the pulsating rhythm of holy joy. Although the outward conditions may remain unchanged for a time, the blessed assurance will come to your heart that you are in the hand of One who understands and who leads His children out of darkness into light.

Yes, when David went into the sanctuary, he began to understand: "Surely thou didst set them in slippery places: thou castedst them down into destruction. How are they brought into desolation, as in a moment! they are utterly consumed with terrors" (verses 18, 19). Now David is beginning to understand that the prosperity of the wicked is only apparent, only a surface prosperity. Their hearts have no peace. Terror stalks their footsteps. They have no sense of security, and they are brought down "in a moment."

Then David laments his own foolishness in verse 22: "So foolish was I, and ignorant: I was as a beast before thee." He acknowledges that he should never have doubted God in the first place and that he should have taken his problems to God for solution at once. He should have trusted in Him to bring him out more than conqueror. At last he understands this and says, "Thou shalt guide me with thy counsel, and afterward receive me to glory. Whom have I in heaven but thee? and there is none upon earth that I desire beside thee. My flesh and my heart faileth: but God is the strength of my heart, and my portion for ever. . . . But it is good for me to draw near to God: I have put my trust in the Lord God, that I may declare all thy works" (verses 24-28).

Of a similar experience, he said in Psalm 37:1-6, "Fret not thyself because of evildoers, neither be thou envious against the workers of iniquity. For they shall soon be cut down like the grass, and wither as the green herb. Trust in the Lord, and do good; so shalt thou dwell in the land, and verily thou shalt be fed. Delight thyself also in the Lord; and he shall give thee the desires of thine heart. Commit thy way unto the Lord; trust also in him; and he shall bring it to pass. And he shall bring forth thy righteousness as the light, and thy judgment as the noonday."

Many of the Christian's problems spring from the fact that his way of life runs counter to the world's way of life. The principles of Christianity run contrary to man's inherent sinfulness, which reveals itself in his works, in the system he has set up, and in the philosophy by which he governs himself. Since Christianity runs counter to all these, it therefore brings the Christian into conflict with the sinner and with his own sinful environment. To such a person trouble is natural. It has always been so, and it will always be so until the kingdoms of this world

become the kingdoms of our Lord. God-fearing people have always had a pretty tough time in this world. They have suffered persecution. "Blessed are ye that hunger now: for ye shall be filled. Blessed are ye that weep now: for ye shall laugh. Blessed are ye, when men shall hate you, and when they shall separate you from their company, and shall reproach you, and cast out your name as evil, for the Son of man's sake. Rejoice ye in that day, and leap for joy: for, behold, your reward is great in heaven: for in the like manner did their fathers unto the prophets" (Luke 6:21-23).

During his captivity in Egypt, Joseph trusted God. H. ARMSTRONG ROBERTS

When Christ Himself came to the earth, he was woefully manhandled and would have gone to His death much earlier had not Heaven intervened. If, then, our Lord and Master could drink the cup of suffering that the world will exact from anyone who lives the Christ-life, we should consider it a privilege to suffer with Him.

"Beloved, think it not strange concerning the fiery trial which is to try you, as though some strange thing happened unto you: but rejoice, inasmuch as ye are partakers of Christ's sufferings; that,

when his glory shall be revealed, ye may be glad also with exceeding joy. If ye be reproached for the name of Christ, happy are ye; for the spirit of glory and of God resteth upon you: on their part he is evil spoken of, but on your part he is glorified. . . . Yet if any man suffer as a Christian, let him not be ashamed; but let him glorify God on this behalf" (1 Peter 4:12-16).

But what possible benefit can come from trouble? Do trials serve any useful purpose at all? Consider the case of Joseph. His brothers unjustly sold him into Egyptian slavery. Upon reaching Egypt, he became a servant in Potiphar's household. Potiphar's wife tried to seduce him, but Joseph ran from her presence. And what did he get for his faithfulness? A term in a dungeon. But did this discourage him? No. Now, if any man had a reason to turn against God, Joseph did. He could have bitterly pitied himself, becoming a rank atheist because he had gotten nothing but tough breaks since the day his jealous brothers had sold him into slavery. But God's hand sheltered him, and God's eye watched over him. Through these trials God prepared this man to share the rulership of the most powerful nation on the face of the earth.

But how could Joseph know that? He simply trusted God, and his trials strengthened that faith. He learned in the damp, dingy dungeon how to trust in God even though everything seemed to go wrong. At the right time God put it all together and brought about a situation that catapulted Joseph from the depth of the dungeon to the throne of Egypt itself. Only then did Joseph understand, and later, as he talked with his brothers about his experiences, he forgave them for selling him into slavery, explaining that God had used them to sell him into slavery so that he might ultimately become master of all Egypt.

Joseph understood the purpose of trial. He had proved his worth in the crucible of affliction, and God Himself judged him worthy of the second-highest trust in the land. And so it is with us. Our faith is tested in order that it may be perfected. Only if we suffer with Christ can we reign with Him. We simply cannot inherit all the joys of the world to come without sacrificing some of the seeming joys that are here. We cannot have both worlds. We must choose one or the other.

Moses made that choice. Of him the Bible says, "By faith Moses, when he was born, was hid three months of his parents, because they saw he was a proper child; and they were not afraid of the king's commandment. By faith Moses, when he was come to years, refused to be called the son of Pharoah's daughter; choosing rather to suffer affliction with the people of God, than to enjoy the pleasures of sin for a season; esteeming the reproach of Christ greater riches than the treasures in Egypt: for he had respect unto the recompence of the reward. By faith he forsook Egypt, not fearing the wrath of the king: for he endured, as seeing him who is invisible" (Hebrews 11:23-27).

And so the refining fires of God separate the dross from the pure metal. Teaching us dependency upon Christ, they enable us to walk through the dark without fear. David could say, "Yea, though I walk through the valley of the shadow of death, I will fear no evil: for thou art with me; thy rod and thy staff they comfort me" (Psalm 23:4). The exceeding joys of the world to come will cause the intensity of present trials to pale into insignificance and will convert sorrow's valley into a vale of rejoicing as they did for the martyrs who, while the flame seared their flesh, sang songs of glory to their Creator and Redeemer.

Power in the Blood

For many years following slavery, a custom was followed that lingers to this day. A man would hire himself out on another's land. He would till a portion of the land for the landowner and the rest for himself. The owner of the farm would supply him with a house to live in, and he could do his trading at the store situated somewhere on the plantation. This became known as "the company store." Many of these transactions were honest, and the tenant farmer made money. However, in all too many cases, after laboring for a year, the tenant farmer would go to settle his accounts, only to find that the charges for groceries and other necessities far exceeded what he had earned. Year after year he would plunge deeper and deeper into debt until he literally "owed his soul to the company store." He was bound by law to continue his service until his debt was paid, and a new form of slavery cropped up.

Each succeeding year found the unfortunate tenant farmer descending to new levels of despair, until at last he gave up all hope of freedom. With dull and listless eyes and with mechanical movements he tilled the soil. To what could he look forward? His deliverance must come from without, or he must toil for the balance of his days in the service of another.

When God created man, He put all things under his dominion. "And God said, Let us make man in our image, after our likeness: and let them have dominion over the fish of the sea, and over the fowl of the air, and over the cattle, and over all the earth, and over every creeping thing that creepeth upon the earth" (Genesis 1:26). As long as man maintained his perfect relationship with God, his work was a pleasure, and he could eat every herb-bearing seed. He was not some hired-out tenant, facing the day-to-day drudgery of working for another. No books contained accounts to burden his mind and to enslave him to the Garden he kept. As a steward of God, Eden was his dominion, his garden, his home, his castle, to keep forever. But the tempter lurked in a nearby tree, determined to change all this by destroying man's happiness and imperiling his relationship with his Maker. He tempted man to doubt God and to take his life into his own hands, to chart a new course, to experiment with transgression, and thus he plunged man and this planet into a darkness from which it has not yet recovered.

Expelled from the Garden, man had to earn his living by the sweat of his brow. Like a prisoner at the bar of justice, he stood judged and condemned. He could not deliver himself. "Having the understanding darkened, being alien-ated from the life of God through the ignorance that is in them, because of the blindness of their heart: who being past feeling have given themselves over unto lascivi-ousness, to work all uncleanness with greediness" (Ephesians 4:18, 19).

"That at that time ye were without Christ, being aliens from the commonwealth of Israel, and strangers from the covenants of promise, having no hope, and without God in

the world" (chapter 2:12).

But "God so loved the world, that he gave his only begotten Son, that whosoever believeth in him should not perish, but have everlasting life. For God sent not his Son into the world to condemn the world; but that the world through him might be saved" (John 3:16, 17).

We need not sit in hopeless frustration because of our sins. We need not suffer the unhappiness that comes with guilt for having transgressed against God. We need not linger in the valley of despondency when above us shines the Star of hope. One fact of history has bred hope in our hearts—the life, death, and resurrection of our Lord Jesus Christ. He was born of the virgin Mary. The angel had said to her, "The Holy Ghost shall come upon thee, and the power of the Highest shall overshadow thee: therefore also that holy thing which shall be born of thee shall be called the Son of God" (Luke 1:35). He was, indeed, the Son of God and the Son of man. We call Him "the God-man," for He was both human and divine. He was as truly human as if He were not divine and yet as truly divine as if He were not human. He was and is the unique Man of history. "And the Word was made flesh, and dwelt among us, (and we beheld his glory, the glory as of the only begotten of the Father,) full of grace and truth" (John 1:14). Through Christ, God the Father provided a means of reconciliation to Himself for mankind. Christ bridged the chasm of sin that separated the creature from his Creator. And now we may, by accepting Him as Lord and Saviour, have fellowship with God as children have with their father.

How does He accomplish this miracle of salvation? "For what the law could not do, in that it was weak through the flesh, God sending his own Son in the likeness of sinful flesh, and for sin, condemned sin in the flesh; that the righteousness of the law might be fulfilled in us, who walk not after the flesh, but after the Spirit" (Romans 8:3, 4).

During His thirty-three years on this earth, His total life condemned all evil. Finally, in a supreme act of mercy He was crucified for our sins. "Christ also hath once suffered for sins, the just for the unjust, that he might bring us to God, being put to death in the flesh, but quickened by the Spirit"(1 Peter 3:18). Yes, He became our substitute in death so that we might share eternal life with Him.

Dr. Chamberlain, a missionary to India, tells of an experience he had while preaching in Benares. Among the devotees who came to bathe in the sacred Ganges River crawled a man who had journeyed wearily on his knees and elbows from a great distance. He hoped that by washing in the sacred stream he would find relief from his troubled heart. Dragging himself to the river's edge, he prayed to Gunga and crept into the water. A moment later he emerged with the old pain still tugging at his heart. As he lay flat on his back in despair, he heard the voice of the missionary. Painfully he raised himself and crawled a little nearer. He listened to the simple story of the cross of Christ. He rose up on his knees, then on his feet, and then clapped his hands and cried, "That's what I want! That's what I want!"

Religious devotees bathing in the sacred Ganges River. © MARCELLO BERTINETTI, PHOTO RESEARCHERS

You see, the story of the cross is the story of redemption, and this poor man needed God's assurance that He would forgive his sins and cleanse his soul—that he could walk in this old, sinful world with hope in his heart. With steady tread and firm footstep, he could wend his way toward the kingdom of God, fully assured that Jesus Christ had died for his sins.

During one of Queen Victoria's journeys, a little boy wanted to see her. He determined to go directly to the castle where she was staying and ask to see her. The sentry at the gate stopped him and inquired what he wanted. "I want to see the queen," the boy said. The soldier laughed at him and with the butt of his musket pushed him away. The boy turned to leave, giving vent to his tears. He had not gone far when he met Prince Albert, who inquired why he was crying. "I want to see the queen," cried the boy, "and that soldier won't let me."

"Won't he? Then come along with me, and I'll take you to the queen," said the prince, taking the lad by the hand. As they approached the guard at the gate, the sentinel, as usual, presented arms to the prince. The boy became terrified and ran away, fearful that the soldier was going to shoot him. The prince soon quieted his fears and led him past the gate into the presence of Her Majesty the Queen, who, surprised, asked her husband whom he had with him. Learning what had happened, she laughed heartily and spoke kindly to the little visitor.

It is even so with Christ. He ushers us into the very presence of the King of the universe and restores fellowship between our souls and the Father. But we must return that matchless love Christ has bestowed upon us. It cannot be a one-sided transaction. It is not enough that God loves us. We must love Him. Romans 5:5 says, "The love of God is shed abroad in our hearts by the Holy Ghost." We do not have to try to love Him. By meditating on His matchless sacrifice for our sins, the shedding of His blood, the way He gave Himself so fully to mankind while here, as well as His present blessings to us, we are led to the feet of Him who gave all heaven for us. We acknowledge His kingship, kinship, and companionship.

As our hearts go out to Him who is our Saviour, we can sing with William Featherstone:

"My Jesus, I love Thee, I know
    Thou art mine;
For Thee all the follies of sin I
    resign;
My gracious Redeemer, my Sav-
    iour art Thou;
If ever I loved Thee, my Jesus,
    'tis now. . . .

"I'll love Thee in life, I will love
    Thee in death,
And praise Thee as long as Thou
    lendest me breath;
And say when the death dew lies
    cold on my brow,
If ever I loved Thee, my Jesus,
    'tis now.

"In mansions of glory and end-
    less delight,
I'll ever adore Thee in heaven so
    bright;
I'll sing with the glittering crown
    on my brow,
If ever I loved Thee, my Jesus,
    'tis now."

Fire Next Time

"Burn, baby, burn" was popularized during the civil disorders in Watts, Harlem, Detroit, Chicago, and Washington, D.C. For a hundred years the blacks protested against racial injustices by nonviolent means. They had progressed from the fiery utterances of Wendel Phillips, Henry Ward Beecher, William Lloyd Garrison, Theodore Parker, and Frederick Douglass to the great compromise enunciated by Booker T. Washington.

However, W. E. B. Du Bois, one of the cofounders of the National Association for the Advancement of Colored People, carried on the earlier tradition. This organization concerned itself mainly with the legal aspects of segregation, understanding clearly that as long as demeaning laws remained on the statute books, there could be no meaningful emancipation.

Then came the student-action groups who staged "sit-ins," "drive-ins," "wade-ins," and "kneel-ins" on the theory that the presentation of a bodily presence without regard to the violence that it attracted would so work on the nation's conscience that it would abolish segregation. Then came Martin Luther King, Jr., with his street marches, boycotts, and other nonviolent assaults on the citadel of discrimination. The combined movements effected a removal of segregation laws from the statute books of the nation so that today, in theory, America is a desegregated country.

The law of the land favors every citizen. However, in all this, a large segment of the hard-core poor were completely bypassed, benefiting little from the national prosperity. An estimated 35 million people in this country live in unbelievable squalor. Children still die from worms, scurvy, beriberi, and pellagra. Thousands of Americans have no access to medical care, and so the poor get poorer while the rich get richer and the middle class get stronger. A rather thick veneer of respectability covered all this until the riots erupted and the dread cry "Burn, baby, burn" echoed through the land.

Investigating committees finally surveyed the situation to give an honest appraisal of the true condition of the hard-core poor. The shocking revelations that followed stung the conscience of the nation, and the government immediately instituted programs to remedy the situation. When it became known that, because of poverty, under privileged children who begin the first grade find it difficult to learn because malnutrition has partially paralyzed their mental capacities, the Head Start program was initiated. In one large Midwestern city alone, forty thousand black people go to bed having had only one meal a day. The woeful inadequacy of the welfare system has now become a byword, for what it offers lasts only for about a half or two thirds of the month in a normal family. Furthermore, the restrictions for the "dole" prevent a man from working, thus destroying his dignity and initiative by creating an attitude of frustration and anger even among the recipients. In short, they become prisoners of welfare.

Then the news reached us that

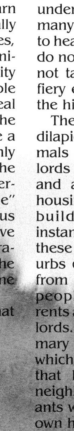

while U.S. farmers each year destroy tons of food in order to maintain the prices of their products, people were starving in the United States of America. A food-stamp program already in operation was vastly liberalized in order to make available government food at a minimum cost to more of the poor. But even this is but a ripple on a vast ocean of poverty and hunger. If the true condition of the inner city ever became widely known and understood, America would divert many of its billions for foreign aid to heal the cancer in its midst. If we do not wake up to this fact, it does not take a prophet to predict the fiery end of the greatest nation in the history of the world.

The core of our cities harbors dilapidated shacks unfit for animals to dwell in. Absentee landlords have been appealed to again and again to bring substandard housing into harmony with city building codes, but, in many instances, inspection is lax; and these landlords living in the suburbs continue to reap rich profits from these shambles, while the people within them pay higher rents and curse their invisible landlords. These are naturally the primary targets for inner-city anger, which accounts for the burnings that have taken place in black neighborhoods. These angry tenants were not burning down "their own homes." They were, they say, eradicating an eyesore, a cancer. They were trying to do something about a problem that nobody has seemed concerned about.

But burning solves few problems, because then our already seriously overcrowded cities have hundreds of homeless people on their hands and no adequate provisions for them. Those who look upon arson as the answer find themselves entrapped by their own solution. This, in turn, increases the anger, the tensions, and the danger of continuing explosions. Only those who have lived through a riot, as the author has, can understand the pain that it inflicts in the ghetto. Community services are disrupted. Innocent babies cannot get milk. Hungry families cannot buy food, since the large chain stores and other sources of food supply are disrupted. Medical services are severely strained. Fear stalks the streets.

In the middle of a holocaust of this nature, thinking men wonder if this solution isn't more painful than the problem. Under conditions of order, there is always the possibility of changing things for the better; but under systems of riot and disorder, everybody hurts. Wars have never settled anything, whether they be between nations, within a nation, or between races of people. It is still true that "all they that take the sword shall perish with the sword." Therefore, we must find a nonviolent solution to the problem of this nation, or we will, by violence, destroy ourselves.

At times, talk seems meaningless and hopeless, yet in the long view, the maintenance of communications between the races is a life and death necessity. Although shocked by the rhetoric of the have-nots, we must still discern beneath it all a basic decency in which justice and humanity mark all the forces of society. The have-nots must prepare themselves to do some listening, too. But their impatience must be understood and accepted, for America has been long on promises and short on delivery. Many seriously question how long they can listen, while America spends billions to send men to the moon, to fight foreign wars, and as foreign aid to other underprivileged countries. The United States alone has 30 million underprivileged people, including Indians, Mexicans, whites, and blacks.

The gospel of the Lord Jesus Christ enjoins the rich to attend to the needs of the poor. It requires the practitioner of our Lord's religion to visit the fatherless and the widows, to feed the hungry, to clothe the naked, to educate the ignorant, to shelter the homeless, to heal the sick, and to feed the impoverished spirits of man with the rich elixir of divine grace. If there is any hope in our world, it lies in the teachings of Scripture and in the thirty-three years of the human manifestation of God on earth in the person of Jesus Christ.

It must be cited as historical fact that, with the coming of Christianity into the world and with its teachings of man's kinship to God and his fellowman, there has come a new sense of decency, dignity, and worth. Wherever slavery has flourished, the condemning finger of Christianity has pointed at it, and the thundering voices of its spokesmen have continually boomed their accusations. Christ gives to each man a new sense of worth and significance that enables him to function hopefully in this present world's atmosphere and that assures him of life in the world to come.

This Far by Faith

A Dutch ship stood offshore at Jamestown, Virginia, on a hot August afternoon. The year was 1619, and aboard huddled twenty blacks later to be exchanged for some New England cookware, rum, and tobacco. They were the first blacks to become residents on the North American continent. We know the names of three of them: Perdo, Isabella, and Anthony. Anthony and Isabella married, and the first black child born on these shores was their son.

But who are the black people in America? What is their background? History records that they are representatives of a once-proud race who inhabited the continent of Africa. We encounter them first in the black and brown tribes of Ethiopia, who joined the people from western Asia and the eastern Mediterranean who were migrating to the area now known as Egypt. Therefore, in those early years there was a curious mixture of people called Egyptians, whom Herodotus described in the fifth century before Christ as being "black and curly haired." Count Volney, who visited Egypt with Napoleon Bonaparte, described the Egyptians as having "sable skin and woolly hair."

Most likely the Egyptians had a variety of appearances as their art depicts, for the migrants came from the east and from the north as well as from black Africa to the south. Each group contributed to the glory of ancient Egypt, and from this fusion of racial stock came the civilization for which Egypt has been so long venerated. During certain periods of Egyptian history, the blacks from the Nubian Desert fully controlled the Egyptian throne. Ra Nahesai, a Negro, intermittently ruled after 1703 B.C. Many Negroes occupied positions of responsibility and honor in the Egyptian government. Nofretari, wife of Ahmose I, Egypt's great imperial leader, has been described as a Negro woman "of great beauty, strong personality, and remarkable administrative

An 1853 German engraving shows a caravan approaching Timbuktu, the intellectual and trading center of the Songhai Empire, one of the mighty Black empires of Africa. From the 1857 book *Travels in Central Africa*, by Barth.

ability." During the Hyksos invasion, from 1700 B.C. to 1580, many Egyptians fled to the Upper Nile Valley and mingled freely with Ethiopians of that region.

The black Pharaoh Piankhi, whose father had seized control of the Upper Nile years earlier, in 741 B.C., completely subjugated Egypt, reducing it to a dependency of Ethiopia for the better part of a century.

Shabaka, Piankhi's brother, took over the leadership in 710 B.C. He maintained peace and sought to repel the Assyrians by negotiation. Succeeding Ethiopian Pharaohs, Shabataka and Tirhakah, also ruled Egypt. Blacks helped construct the sphinxes, pyramids, and public buildings of Egypt. Under Tirhakah new buldings were contructed at Tanis, Memphis, and Thebes, as well as a great temple at Karnak. Prosperity was so extensive under Tirhakah that he styled himself "the emperor of the world."

Then there were the black African states of Ghana, Melle, and Songhay. European scholars came for advanced study to a black African university at Timbuktu. Under these and twelve lesser empires, Africa achieved such a state of civilized excellence that horses were bedded down in silk and tethered with silken cords.

But the end of these empires and the arrival of Europeans assured the decline of Africa. It is understandable in view of the rigors of the slave trade, which robbed this continent of untold millions of the flower of its inhabitants, for the slaveholders sought only the best and the heartiest. However, when the European arrived in Africa, he still found evidences of civilization, although in some areas it was more pronounced than in others. He found the Pygmies manufacturing bark cloth and fiber baskets. The Hottentots devoted much time and attention to making clothing from textiles, skins, and furs. The Ashanti on the Gold Coast glazed pottery and wove rugs with considerable skill. Many of the Sudanese manufactured wooden tools and implements.

But the slave trade practically depopulated the continent of its most promising manhood and womanhood, and those who survived the terror of the "middle passage," as the trip across the ocean was known, were subjected to every imaginable indignity from flogging to selling members of families into separate states, thus destroying the unity of the home.

With millions of their black brothers in the Caribbean, twenty blacks were introduced on this continent in 1619. This number grew until it finally reached millions. Traffic in human flesh became the backbone of the New World's economy. Large companies like the East India Company organized to foster slave trading. For 240 years slavery persisted in America, and the only social life that the Negro had was church, the only book he could own was the Bible, and the only lecturer permitted was the preacher. But the Bible fired the black man's hopes for freedom.

In addition, thousands of white men, first in England and later in America, lifted their voices against the slave trade. Then came the Civil War, during which thousands of whites died for the emancipation of the blacks. Of the 200,000 black men who fought in the same war for their own freedom, 38,000 lost their lives. Their gallantry was a

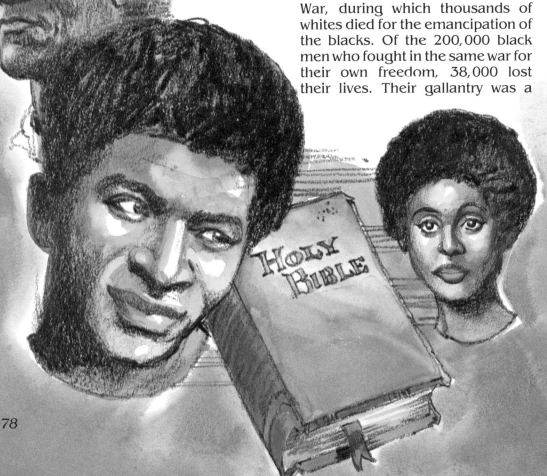

thing noticed by their commanders and historians. General Ulysses S. Grant paid particular tribute to them for their fighting around Richmond and Petersburg.

Then Abraham Lincoln signed the Emancipation Proclamation in 1863. The passage of the Thirteenth and the Fourteenth Amendments of the Constitution eventually ensured the freedom of the black man and his participation in American government. Steady progress has marked the past century in America in spite of the fact that segregation laws specifically designed to demean, degrade, and debase him were hastily instituted after slavery. The black man, aided by concerned whites and the Federal government, continued his upward march. Educational institutions were established. Black men went into business, the arts, the sciences, and government. They qualified as lawyers, judges, doctors, nurses, social workers, and artisans in the trades. The churches flourished as ministers of God, hailing the new freedom, continued to inspire the black man onward and upward.

The National Association for the Advancement of Colored People spearheaded the battle in the courts; and we entered the Martin Luther King, Jr., era where nonviolent demonstrations sought immediate implementation of the Constitution of the United States with the result that today the laws of the land outlaw segregation in any part of this country. Attitudes toward granting the black man full freedom as a citizen in this country have softened.

We now face the enormous task of reaching the estimated 20 million blacks and whites whom the industrial revolution bypassed. Locked in a cycle of poverty, yet surrounded by plenty, they constitute the major challenge of government and people. Indeed, the survival of this nation may well depend on what we do now for those less fortunate in the land of the free and the home of the brave. Churches, banks, industry, schools, and government must combine to wipe the blight of poverty and ignorance from the face of this land. We have the power and resources to do it. Do we have the will? Our right to survive as a world leader hinges on our commitment here.

Jesus said a long time ago, "As ye would that men should do to you, do ye also to them" (Luke 6:31). Paul said that the strong must bear the infirmities of the weak. And while these agencies must combine to uplift the poor, both black and white, we must recognize there is a stirring in the black neighborhoods of this nation—a sense of worth, a sense of significance, and a sense of one's own contribution to the birth of the nation. We must guide this new sense of dignity into constructive channels of self-help and self-confidence. We must fight the despair that is rapidly gripping this country. "We've come this far by faith, leaning on the Lord." We cannot leave our faith now.

Christ is the source of our power; and black, white, red, and yellow need His power now more than ever before. With it and with Him, we may face a future that outshines a million suns. Without Him, the future is blacker than a thousand midnights.

Break
Bread Together

This century may be properly labeled "the century of the angry man." Crimes of violence commonly occur. Among both the children and the aged, unbridled temper holds sway. A mysterious and unnatural anger pervades men and nations. The feverish intensity of these times has in some way affected everything and everybody.

Our own nation has come to one of the severest crises in its history. Not since the Revolutionary War and the Civil War have Americans stood to lose so much. Thousands are talking, but few are listening, while the cities of America are on the critical list. People who have waited for more than three hundred years for their constitutionally guaranteed freedoms are being arrogantly told to wait longer. Little wonder the disadvantaged shout back, "Freedom now!"

The great majority of Americans feel threatened by the black minority. In the past ten years there has been an abnormal sale of guns and other instruments of death. The police forces of the cities have trained for warfare in the streets. Many of them have ordered armored cars for the racial eruptions they feel will surely come. In the meantime, the pattern of demonstrations shifted from the streets to the nation's high school and college campuses. Those protests transcended racial lines. Clearly the students on our campuses were thoroughly disenchanted with the twentieth-century version of the American dream. They had their own solutions, which may or may not solve; and their own answers, which may or may not answer; but the current apprehension and outright fear of citizen for citizen does not speak well for the future of the country. We are playing a game of racial roulette. And our nation, strong as it is, can destroy itself with its own frustrations and fears.

The greatest danger to freedom lies not in the mammoth armies that may oppose us but in the spiritual poverty so evident among us, resulting in the apparent disin-

The time has come for men and women of all races and ethnic groups to break bread together. DAVID B. SHERWIN

81

tegration of the very fabric of our society. If we will survive at all, we must "cool it" now. It would pay us all to pause and reexamine the goals of our society and cast overboard the dead weights of racial prejudice, animosity, and discriminatory practices.

We must remember that nothing in history can encourage us that we shall ultimately reach this ideal. All past civilizations have been built on the prostrate forms of the oppressed and have ultimately come crashing down to the earth under their own weight of corruption. Must we go the way of all flesh? While there is time, let us, white and black, ponder the question of our common destiny. Three things are sure: first, we cannot exist independently of each other on the same continent and both survive; second, one race cannot enslave the other and retain its own liberties; third, there can be no security against an outside foe in a nation divided against itself.

I can, therefore, see no reason in a white man who will allow his prejudice against blacks to exceed his love for the security of his country. Nor can I ascribe reason to any black who would so hate white men that he would destroy himself to even the score.

Our nation has already seen the fruits of violence. Since the Emancipation Proclamation, whites have lynched five thousand blacks. Conversely, within recent years we have seen black anger spill over into the streets with the subsequent sacrifice of lives and property. But neither the lynching of blacks by whites nor the destruction of property by blacks has positively improved the economic, social, political, or spiritual lives of either. Someone has said, "In conditions of order we may have justice and injustice, but in conditions of disorder we can only have injustice." However, neither situation is ideal. Those who wield the power must understand that law and order are acceptable only when accompanied by justice. Any peace sustained by mere force of arms is a false peace.

Every individual citizen, black and white, must totally commit himself to the betterment of all mankind, but he must base his commitment on principles of morality. This implies the recognition of the kinship of all men to God and to each other. For man to try to act as if God does not exist is sheer self-delusion. The existence of the universe, of this planet, and of man himself indicates that there is a God. It is more sensible to deny one's own existence than to close one's eyes to the overwhelming evidence of God's presence in the universe.

Man is related to God by creation. "And the Lord God formed man of the dust of the ground, and breathed into his nostrils the breath of life; and man became a living soul" (Genesis 2:7). There is, therefore, a love relationship, a moral obligation, on the part of man to return to God the respect and love due Him. Man can demonstrate this love for God by exercising the self-control required of him by his Creator-Father, by worshiping and adoring Him as the Lord of the universe, and by accepting His character of love in place of his own hate and selfishness. Thus, with all

our hearts, minds, and spirits we can give ourselves to our Creator-God.

The second principle of God's law of love requires, "Thou shalt love thy neighbour as thyself" (Leviticus 19:18). Love, the most powerful force in the world, makes friends of our enemies. That is why Jesus said, "Love your enemies, bless them that curse you, do good to them that hate you" (Matthew 5:44). It is still true that "all they that take the sword shall perish with the sword" (chapter 26:52). Therefore, America's racial minority is courting suicidal disaster to take up arms in hope that by force it may achieve its constitutionally guaranteed freedoms.

The white majority can take no comfort in this fact, for while blacks cannot hope to achieve ultimate freedom through force of arms, neither may whites destroy ideas of freedom with bullets. So numerous are blacks in this nation today that they cannot be destroyed by force of arms without this entire nation going up in flames, nor may the majority deprive the minority of its freedom without oppressing themselves.

The only path for national survival lies in the direction of love and nonviolence, and both whites and blacks must resolve, in the language of the emancipator, that "this government cannot endure permanently, half slave and half free." In the name and spirit of our Lord Jesus Christ, "let us all get together with the Lord. Let us all get together with the Lord and treat each other like sisters and brothers. Let us all get together with the Lord." Only then will this nation, conceived in liberty and dedicated to the proposition that all men are created equal and endowed by their Creator with the inalienable rights of life, liberty, and the pursuit of happiness, abandon the gray shades of hypocrisy for the brilliant sunlight of sterling example. Only then will the flame that burns eternally in the upraised hand of the Statue of Liberty proclaim in fact what it has in theory, that this land, indeed, is a haven for the oppressed and a refuge for the downtrodden.

By and By—
Think of That

When something is so glorious that it defies description, the phrase heard in the ghetto is "Out of sight, man. Out of sight." But any promise by man to man pales into insignificance when compared with God's promises to all who, by faith, accept His Son as Saviour.

From time to time human governments have held forth great promises to their citizens—promises that did not take into consideration the basic selfishness of human nature and hence man's reluctance to share power, wealth, and culture with those less fortunate. Nor did they recognize human pride, which, when it has achieved itself and denied certain privileges to others, assumes self superior to others by virtue of the then-existent status level. Human pride is blind and, therefore, not susceptible to the cure offered it by history. The plain record of humanity on this earth reveals one race of men dominating the global scene only to be replaced by another and then another so that the myth of natural superiority collapses on the sharp end of human history.

Is there any place in the universe where all men may find the fullest satisfaction in living? Thank God, the Bible indicates that such a place exists, and it is really "out of sight." The apostle Paul makes it clear that there is nothing permanent about this world: "Here have we no continuing city, but we seek one to come" (Hebrews 13:14). It is not wrong to seek a better country than any found on this earth, and Hebrews 11:13-16 clearly indicates that we do not seek that City in vain. "These all died in faith, not having received the promises, but having seen them afar off, and were persuaded of them, and embraced them, and confessed that they were strangers and pilgrims on the earth. For they that say such things declare plainly that they seek a country. . . . But now they desire a better country, that is, an heavenly: wherefore God is not ashamed to be called their God: for he hath prepared for them a city."

Of Abraham the Bible says, "He looked for a city which hath foundations, whose builder and maker is God" (verse 10). And Hebrews 12:22 proclaims, "Ye are come unto mount Sion, and unto the city of the living God, the heavenly Jerusalem, and to an innumerable company of angels." The author of Hebrews calls it a "heavenly city," meaning that it isn't anywhere on this earth. When Jesus went there, He left the earth. "Ye men of Galilee, why stand ye gazing up into heaven? this same Jesus, which is taken up from you into heaven, shall so come in like manner as ye have seen him go into heaven" (Acts 1:11).

After I preached a sermon on this once, a man asked, "When is up down and down up, and how may we know the exact direction in which Christ went?" My answer to him was that the only thing we need to know is that he went "off" the earth, and, therefore, we may search this world from center to circumference and not find that City. This is the important thing. Fortunately, the Bible gives a description of that City. "And I John saw the holy city, new Jerusalem, coming down from God out of heaven, prepared as a bride adorned for her husband. And I heard a great voice out of heaven saying, Behold, the tabernacle of God is with men, and he will dwell with them, and they shall be his people, and God himself shall be with them, and be their God" (Revelation 21:2, 3).

Not only is there a City out there somewhere, but here we read the startling announcement that this City will come to this earth, and God will live with men in it. What a change that will make! God will take up His proper position as the Ruler of this planet and put down the usurper, that old serpent called the devil and Satan, destroying him and his followers in a lake of fire.

"And in the days of these kings shall the God of heaven set up a kingdom, which shall never be destroyed: and the kingdom shall not be left to other people, but it shall break in pieces and consume all these kingdoms, and it shall stand for ever" (Daniel 2:44). The New Jerusalem, capital city of our God, is most glorious. "And he carried me away in the spirit to a great and high mountain, and shewed me that great city, the holy Jerusalem, descending out of heaven from God, having the glory of God: and her light was like unto a stone most precious, even like a jasper stone, clear as crystal; and

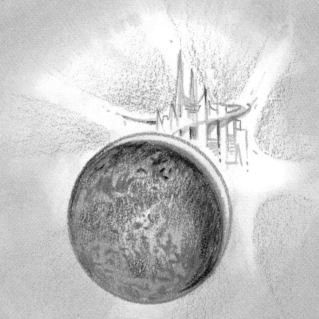

had a wall great and high, and had twelve gates, and at the gates twelve angels, and names written thereon, which are the names of the twelve tribes of the children of Israel: on the east three gates; on the north three gates; on the south three gates; and on the west three gates. And the wall of the city had twelve foundations, and in them the names of the twelve apostles of the Lamb" (Revelation 21:10-14). The wall is of jasper according to verse 18, the gates are pearl, and the street is gold, according to verse 21. An angel measured the City. It is almost fourteen hundred miles around—slightly under the combined size of Arizona and Connecticut.

Yes, we shall be free at last from air pollution, water pollution, scorching deserts, asphalt streets, concrete jungles, falling plaster, invading rats, and garbage-littered alleys. "And God shall wipe away all tears from their eyes; and there shall be no more death, neither sorrow, nor crying, neither shall there be any more pain: for the former things are passed away" (verse 4).

But not everyone will enter that City. "For without are dogs, and sorcerers, and whoremongers, and murderers, and idolaters, and whosoever loveth and maketh a lie" (chapter 22:15). "And he that sat upon the throne said, Behold, I make all things new. And he said unto me, Write: for these words are true and faithful. And he said unto me, It is done. I am Alpha and Omega, the beginning and the end. I will give unto him that is athirst of the fountain of the water of life freely. He that overcometh shall inherit all things; and I will be his God, and he shall be my son" (chapter 21:5-7).

A young boy visiting with a wise old man said to him, "Sir, I want to know the best of two worlds."

"You ask too much, young man," replied the wise man, "for you can have only the best of one."

"That's just it," replied the youngster. "I must know the best of two in order to choose which one."

Of course, the old man was right. We cannot have this world and the world to come, too. We must choose one or the other. But the young man was also right. Without knowledge of the two, we cannot make an intelligent choice. However, God has told us about both and has encouraged us to make the better choice.

An old peanut vendor in a downpour was trying to sell his soaked sacks of peanuts. "Peanuts for sale. Peanuts for sale," he shouted.

One man, sloshing by, stopped to ask, "Say, man, isn't this a terrible day to be selling peanuts?"

"Yes," replied the peanut vendor, "but by and by, think of that." Yes, by and by the sun would shine. It could not always rain.

Said the psalmist, "Weeping may endure for a night, but joy cometh in the morning" (Psalm 30:5). And the old slave sang, "By and by when the morning comes and the saints of God will soon go gathering home, We'll tell the story of how we overcame and will understand it better, by and by." And yet another sang, "There will be no more sorrow, no tomorrow, No more sighing and no more crying, For we will bid farewell to this earthly care and wipe our weeping eye."

The Earth Is the Lord's

I had entered a printing shop to place an ad in the daily newspaper. When I returned, I noticed that my coat had disappeared from the front seat of my car. Seeing a gentleman standing nearby reading the paper, I approached him and asked, "Did you see anyone steal my coat from the front seat of my car?"

"No," he said, "I didn't."

"Well, did you see anybody take it?"

"Yes, I did."

I asked him how he distinguished between taking and stealing.

"Oh," he said, "that's easy. For hundreds of years, our people have been exploited. The employers have withheld the best jobs from them and, by common consent, kept their salaries generally low. So what he did was not stealing but reclaiming—a partial payment of the general debt owed us for present and past grievances."

Now, the man knew his history. For more than two hundred years black people have, indeed, suf-fered under inhumane treatment. They have toiled, but have received inadequate payment. It is equally true that at times both the Federal and State governments have been reluctant to do anything to bring relief. In recent years, however, this has changed. Government has realized a greater sense of responsibility and has offered on-the-job training with payment for those who want to learn a specific skill. Although this is little and late, it is a change for the better. While we cannot deny that some of the social disorders have hastened the change in attitude on the part of those in power, we must also add that many of these people have wanted to change for years and thus welcome this opportunity to demonstrate their basic goodwill. The system can be made to work for the benefit of all men if we bend our energies more fervently in this direction. It is too late and too dangerous to start a new country and to experiment with unfamiliar ideologies. We have this country

When Douglas Johnson returned $240,000 that he had found, people said he was crazy. UPI/BETTMANN NEWSPHOTOS

and system, and we can make them work for all of us. In this we dare not fail.

But what of the man who stole my coat? I, too, am black. I had not exploited him. Here we have another illustration of the blindness of racial prejudice. He assumed that the automobile standing in front of the printing shop and the coat inside of it formed part of a system that had "taken him for a ride," and he determined to "even the score." However, there is such a thing as basic honesty. When a man takes that which does not belong to him, he is stealing—the race of the victim notwithstanding. We cannot cover up this fact with high-sounding words such as *reclamation.* Nor does the rationale stand up that I am entitled to my brother's goods by virtue of past or present "exploitation." While exloitation may form the basis for both government and industry doing more than they have done in the past to heal the wounds of black America, it certainly does not constitute a reason for stealing.

God dedicated a whole commandment of the Decalogue to this sin: "Thou shalt not steal" (Exodus 20:15). The Bible also speaks of dealing fairly, honestly, and justly with our fellowman—a clear obligation for both blacks and whites. Furthermore, dishonesty is not the exclusive property of any one race. As we read government statistics on theft, we notice that the highest rates involve black people in the ghettos. Yet we must not ignore the fact that the major bank robberies, the embezzlement of millions of dollars, and the dishonesty of public officials in high places involve citizens of the white communities. Nor can we forget that a large section of the northeastern part of the United States was sold by the unsuspecting Indians for a box of worthless beads, and there is no thought of restitution. We may also add that the 240 years of unrequited toil exacted from black people constitute the greatest theft in our nation's history. But as my father used to tell me when I was a boy, "Son, nothing that has ever happened to me or to you would justify your taking that which doesn't belong to you."

Another sickness going these days in America's cities has infected even teenagers—kleptomania. They steal for sheer "kicks." Things have gotten so bad that it isn't safe even to go away and leave your home. Large trucks back up and empty houses of all valuable furnishings. If your automobile stalls and you leave it by the road overnight, by the next day it is likely to be stripped of all its valuable parts.

Stealing can be done in other ways, too. High interest rates contribute to the rich getting richer and the poor getting poorer. Slick business deals that yield larger profits than warranted are hailed as "blessings from the Lord." It is said that some of our most brilliant citizens are now in prisons, because somewhere down in their characters they lacked the element of basic honesty.

In March, 1961, Douglas Johnson, a black custodial worker, found $240,000, which he returned to its owner. Of the letters he received from the public, 25 percent suggested he was crazy, revealing to some extent the poverty of spirit that has now beset many. An elderly former neighbor of mine had deposited all his savings in a bank. One day two flim-flam artists knocked on his door and went to work on him, and within a few minutes my friend, under an almost hypnotic trance, went to the bank, withdrew his money, and handed it to the strangers. He never heard from them again.

"Gold! gold! gold! gold!
Bright and yellow, hard and cold,
Molten, graven, hammered and rolled,
Heavy to get, and light to hold;

Hoarded, bartered, bought and
 sold,
Stolen, borrowed, squandered,
 doled:
Spurned by the young, but
 hugged by the old
To the very verge of the church-
 yard mold;
Price of many a crime untold."
 —Thomas Hood

It is said that the Civil War left Robert E. Lee a poor man. The Louisiana lottery offered him ten thousand dollars a year simply for the use of his name, but he replied, "My name is all that I have left, and that is not for sale."

Men deal dishonestly not only with one another but also with God. "Will a man rob God? Yet ye have robbed me. But ye say, Wherein have we robbed thee? In tithes and offerings. Ye are cursed with a curse: for ye have robbed me, even this whole nation. Bring ye all the tithes into the storehouse, that there may be meat in mine house, and prove me now herewith, saith the Lord of hosts, if I will not open you the windows of heaven, and pour you out a blessing, that there shall not be room enough to receive it. And I will rebuke the devourer for your sakes, and he shall not destroy the fruits of your ground; neither shall your vine cast her fruit before the time in the field, saith the Lord of hosts. And all nations shall call you blessed: for ye shall be a delightsome land, saith the Lord of hosts" (Malachi 3:8-12).

The word *tithe* means "tenth part." Not only does God claim one seventh of our time for worship, but He also claims one tenth of our income to support His work in the earth. The gospel commission which Jesus gave to His disciples in Matthew 28:19, 20 must be carried out, and God has ordained the tithing system for the support of His worldwide ministry.

Few people feel a personal obligation to support God's work in the earth, however, and they have every right to know that God calls them robbers. But look at the benefits He promises to those who will faithfully and honestly share their financial and material blessings. The requirement to tithe helps one develop spiritually, because it is impossible to be selfish and to faithfully carry out God's command. The whole gospel of the Lord Jesus Christ aims for character development, and the very core of love is unselfishness, whereas the very core of sin is selfishness. Christ will eradicate selfishness from the heart. "If any man will come after me, let him deny himself, and take up his cross, and follow me" (Matthew 16:24).

Nothing more accurately measures a man's spirit of self-denial than what he does with his money. Said Jesus, "Where your treasure is, there will your heart be also" (chapter 6:21). Someone has said that the man who has lived for himself has the privilege of being his own mourner when he dies. The total focus of Christ's life on earth was self-abnegation: "I am meek and lowly in heart: and ye shall find rest unto your souls" (chapter 11:29). Christ, King of the universe, stooped to the position of a man so that men might be exalted to share in God's glory. We all can arise to new heights in Christ Jesus by exhibiting His lowliness of character.

The Wages of Sin

"But God commendeth his love toward us, in that, while we were yet sinners, Christ died for us" (Romans 5:8).

Until Lucifer sinned, all was perfect harmony in the universe, but the double transgression of Adam and Eve further shattered this peaceful atmosphere. With the sounding of this discordant note, angels began writing a new and fatal chapter on human history in the record books of God. Because of the seriousness of transgression, God had to pay the highest price to redeem man.

We must recognize sin for what it is—rebellion against God. Joseph recognized this. When Potiphar's wife propositioned him, Joseph asked, "How then can I do ths great wickedness, and sin against God?" (Genesis 39:9). And the psalmist cried, "Against thee, thee only, have I sinned, and done this evil in thy sight: that thou mightest be justified when thou speakest, and be clear when thou judgest" (Psalm 51:4).

Sin as rebellion against God is highly personal and destroys the relationship between God and man. "If I regard iniquity in my heart, the Lord will not hear me" (Psalm 66:18). "But your iniquities have separated between you and your God, and your sins have hid his face from you, that he will not hear" (Isaiah 59:2).

So we see God's view of sin. It involves more than breaking rules. It insults God Himself. It breaks God's heart of love. The sinner is on a collision course with the Almighty. This is why sin is so serious. "Whosoever committeth sin transgresseth also the law: for sin is the transgression of the law" (1 John 3:4). To go contrary to God's basic rules for harmony in the universe is to commit sin, and sin is contrary to all nature.

Human rebellion cannot change divine nature, but it has drastically changed environmental nature. "And unto Adam he said, Because thou hast hearkened unto the voice of thy wife, and hast eaten of the tree, of which I commanded thee, saying, Thou shalt not eat of it: cursed is the ground for thy sake; in sorrow shalt thou eat of it all the days of thy life; thorns also and thistles shall it bring forth to thee; and thou shalt eat the herb of the field; in the sweat of thy face shalt thou eat bread, till thou return unto the ground; for out of it wast thou taken: for dust thou art, and unto dust shalt thou return" (Genesis 3:17-19).

"The earth also is defiled under the inhabitants thereof; because they have transgressed the laws, changed the ordinance, broken the everlasting covenant. Therefore hath the curse devoured the earth, and they that dwell therein are desolate: therefore the inhabitants of the earth are burned, and few men left" (Isaiah 24:5, 6).

Sin is against God, against His law, against environmental nature, and against man. When we walk contrary to the laws of the universe, we are working against our own best interests. When man is out of harmony with God, he is in conflict with himself. No wonder emotional instability is rampant in our world! Increasing mental disorders pose a major problem to the human family. "To thine own self be true," a philosophical truism with a Biblical basis, has its credibility rooted in the very nature of man. When a man sins, he sins not only against others but against himself. Even if one simply, say, becomes a drunkard, he sins against humanity, because he robs the human family of the potential blessing he might provide for the needy.

Sin offends God, who must deal with the rebellion that has appeared in His universe. What would God do with the emergency? The answer: Somebody had to die. "Behold, all souls are mine; as the soul of the father, so also the soul of the son is mine: the soul that sinneth, it shall die" (Ezekiel 18:4). The sinner lived under the death decree. The safety of the universe demanded his execution. If he was to be saved, God had to devise a plan which would satisfy the law and extend pardon to the guilty sinner. Well in advance of this emergency God had laid a plan for saving sinners. Its foundations lay deep in the very nature of God and, therefore, can never be fully explained. The plan to save man was born of love. "For God so loved the world, that he gave his only begotten Son, that whosoever believeth in him should not perish, but have everlasting life" (John 3:16).

The plan of salvation satisfied the claims of the law by providing a substitute for man in death. "The wages of sin is death; but the gift of God is eternal life through Jesus Christ our Lord" (Romans 6:23). Sin has no other wages. It can pay off with no other money. Spiritual death, physical death, and eternal death are its sure rewards. The spiritually dead, or living dead, have allowed sin to dominate them. They have despised the high privilege of repentance, faith, and confession. While alive physically, they failed to drink deeply from the fountain of life, and therefore their spiritual nature died. This is one of the wages of sin.

Physical death also reminds us that the wages of sin is death. All over the land, every day and every

Death is a result of sin's entering our world. MEYLAN THORESEN

hour, mourners, clothed in black, slowly trudge the last feet to someone's final resting place.

Then there is the final and ultimate destruction of the wicked that we call "eternal death," meaning death from which there will be no resurrection. Such is the penalty of sin. Such is the seriousness of transgressing God's law.

But what of the price of redemption? Would divine justice accept a man for a man? an angel for a man? God for man? The law itself requires the man committing the sin to pay the penalty, but if a substitute is to be found, where must he come from and why? Certainly a man substituting for man would be unacceptable, for nowhere on earth is there a man worthy to atone for the sins of another man. "All have sinned, and come short of the glory of God" (chapter 3:23). Certainly a sinner could not atone for a sinner. Under the provisions of the Levitical service, the lamb that substituted for sinful man had to be "without spot," and there just aren't any such men around, nor have there been any since Adam fell.

But what about an angel for a man? Would this meet the requirements of divine justice? Since an angel tempted Adam and Eve to sin, might not an angel redeem man, thus atoning for both the sin of angels and of men? The reasoning seems logical, but it has one weakness. It does not reckon with God's love, a love so total in its comprehension of man's needs that it will allow no one else to assume this fearful responsibility. It must give of itself for man's sins. God must answer the devil. God's love must prove itself as sufficient as His justice is exacting. Under these terms, no less a person than God Himself could atone for man's sins.

The great Creator became our Saviour, and He who was the very fullness of the Godhead put His life on the line for the sins of man. By this act He satisfied the claims of divine justice for all who will believe in Him and accept his sacrifice. Further, Christ lived a perfect life, and this He shares with every believing child of God. By shedding His blood, He has provided the means for cleansing from the crimson stain of trangression, and by His resurrection He has assured us of ultimate triumph over death—an eternal life and a glorious hereafter. He who created man, redeemed him, thus answering forever the age-old charge that a God who knew man would sin before He created him could not possibly love him. The deepest manifestation of love would not be a failure to create but a willingness to redeem, and Christ's life on earth and death on Calvary's cross provided God's unanswerable argument of love. God's unselfish sharing of Himself with man gives all criticism of His love a hollow ring. Angels understand this and marvel that sin-blinded men fail to comprehend it.

The Bottom Rail

As a boy I often heard the expression "The bottom rail is coming to the top" used in black neighborhoods. It signified the blackman's unwillingness to remain content in his subservient role. It said that he would not "stay in his place." It solemnly promised to all concerned that whatever privileges came to citizens of these United States would one day come to him, the black man, the former slave. Black men used to encourage one another with these words: "The bottom rail will come to the top."

I think of my childhood neighborhood, an area sealed off from the white community, not by a visible Berlin-type wall but by an invisible curtain of prejudice that was evident, although not visible as such to the eye. We always knew when we had crossed the line into hostile territory. During certain times at night we were just not seen in those areas on foot. Today, the white man experiences the same fear in certain ghetto areas. Yet when I was a boy, he could walk unhindered through any neighborhood with the absolute assurance that no one would touch him.

One of the prime fears of little boys growing up in the ghetto was that of "going to jail." Every young man strongly suspected that at one time or another he would run afoul of the law and be jailed. As I ponder the crime statistics today, I can't help wondering just what might have happened had not this bitter hopelessness reflected itself in the thinking of so many ghetto youth. A people rejected by society and turned in upon themselves tend to destroy themselves in the midst of an atmosphere of inevitable doom. There is an individual feeling of inevitability toward the "white man's law" and its enforcement. If law enforcement agencies could come to grips with this feeling, they would solve much of the crime problem. Fortunately, community relations programs—where the officers become the big brothers, playmates, and helpers of the

95

youth—are now being inaugurated.

Saturday night in the ghetto has always been a crucial night. I can remember the sights, sounds, and smells of the neighborhood on Saturday evenings. In a nearby honky-tonk the jukebox would blare its baleful sound. A block away a group of eight people would sit around a table on which stood a kerosene lamp. They were "note singing." On another corner a church would sponsor a fish-sandwich sale. Nearby, a believer in private enterprises would barbecue over an open pit filled with live coals. Wearing an apron liberally besmudged with grease and blood, he would frequently smear the meat with a mysterious sauce of his own concoction. Occasionally he would slice off a piece of the barbecue for a customer.

Saturday night in the ghetto! A night when violence erupts, a pistol cracks, and the ambulances wail. The inevitable has happened. The hot summer night's atmosphere carries the mingled odors of frying fish, roasting barbecue, and flowing liquor. Saturday night—when the wise stay indoors, while the foolish stagger heedlessly to the cold death march of the damned. Saturday night in the ghetto! Police cars cruise slowly while suspicious eyes dart about in search of an offender.

The bottom rail; could it come to the top? This was the question of yesteryear, when no black man could play organized baseball, when basketball was a white man's sport and golf had the same restrictions, when Hollywood in its search for actors and actresses completely bypassed the blacks or else used them in demeaning roles.

Only a trickle of blacks finished high school and ventured into college. The NAACP was the lone voice in the wilderness pleading that white society give the man on the bottom rail a chance. But the great bulk of blacks were purposeful, forward-looking, hopeful, and education thirsty. Like my father, many parents worked at two or three jobs at once to see that their children received a better education than theirs. We blacks played stick ball in the streets, made basketball hoops of worn-out bushel baskets, and used great wads of paper for the ball. I saw would-be pitchers aim their balls straight at a target on the side of a house. When those balls landed, they landed loud, usually bringing forth a mother or an irate aunt, who put an end to such primitive modes of practice that would increase the depreciation of the home.

But the bottom rail was on the move, and look at it now! Twenty million of the 30 million blacks in this country have now achieved "middle class" status. The industrial revolution has not passed them by, and they now have an economic base. They are educating their children. Now they can vote. Black men walk the halls of Congress and occupy important positions in the executive branch of government. We now have the privilege of access to public services such as motels, restrooms, and restaurants. That mention should be made of this at all should be embarrassing, but does it not reflect the progress of the bottom rail and the evolution in the thinking of the top rail?

The economic curtain is now under assault. Blacks appear as clerks in stores where formerly only whites could work. Labor unions are being pried open. Businesses operating in black neighborhoods now employ black personnel and form black partnerships. The bottom rail has moved nearer the top. Black educators occupy positions of trust and respect on the faculties of our nation's schools. Black students, in increasing numbers, now attain the highest degrees in the land. Police departments are following the enlightened policy of hiring blacks to do patrol duty and of giving them open privileges to work up through the ranks. Blacks excel in the sports of basketball, football, and baseball. There are blacks in golf, and recently the foremost tennis player in America was black. The movie industry, recognizing this trend, has given increasing emphasis to black participation.

No doubt the changes have not taken place fast enough nor gone far enough, but only the blind would deny that changes for the better have taken place in this country. But our challenge as a nation today is the 8 to 10 million blacks and 15 million whites and Mexicans whom the industrial revolution has completely bypassed.

This is also the hour for the witness of the church. Tremendous issues now confront us, and cowardice must not mute Christ's witness through His church. The underprivileged millions must also hear God's voice and see His healing. They must be made aware that somebody loves them. This is not the day of the do-gooder. It is not the day for men who wish to quiet their consciences. It is the day when brother feels love and responsibility for brother. The underprivileged must be brought into the mainstream. The rehabilitative powers of the gospel must be brought to bear on the total man. Already we see miracles in the ghetto. The unmotivated are beginning to live meaningfully and significantly, contributing to the total enrichment of life.

Men on the bottom rail must not overlook what they can do themselves to move toward the top. They must study God's Word. They must exercise their privilege of prayer. Faith in God must be the cornerstone of their motivation, and love for their fellowman must pervade their every human contact. Meanwhile, those who have must understand that one man's hunger affects us all. One man's sickness infects us all. If one man is uneducated, his ignorance diminishes me. Let us, therefore, move together into the future, bearing each other's burdens and sharing each other's joys.

Jesus gives us freedom from the slavery of habit and vice.

Freedom

Uhuru means "freedom," and freedom lies at the foundation of this nation. The Pilgrims sought these shores in flight from religious and civil oppression, and our Founding Fathers established this nation upon the philosophy that all men are entitled to "life, liberty, and the pursuit of happiness." An intensive concern with liberty and freedom has marked the nearly four hundred years of this country's history. Having begun in pursuit of freedom, our nation must constantly redefine it with reference to both its majority and minority citizens. Obviously, freedom must have its contrasting state, namely, slavery or semislavery, and there must be some dividing line, some standard, by which to measure freedom.

In terms of civil freedom, liberty without moral or legal restraints can lead only to chaos, and fear will rule a society where might makes right. This is the law of the jungle, and thousands today have the caveman's complex. In rebellion against the evils of a faulty human society, they withdraw themselves to the hills, attending only to their elementary needs in a vain search for a peace that continues to elude them. In rebelling against the evils of society, they have also thrown overboard its virtues. Their unbathed bodies and unkempt persons give rise to a stench as obnoxious as the evils they protest. For instance, America's open housing law, which entitles a man to purchase property whenever his money is adequate, has been interpreted as a basic freedom. Others, however, feel threatened by this. They say that a man should be free to choose his neighbors. These positions are irreconcilable, with the result that the man with money purchases in a neighborhood where he is not wanted, and the man who thinks he has the right to choose his neighbors sells his property and goes to a new neighborhood. But where can this end? If the man with money has the freedom to buy where he pleases, it is only a matter of time before someone buys into the new neighborhood to which the former owner has fled.

Man without God cannot possibly define freedom, because freedom is spiritual in nature, and only when we recognize this can we administer it with justice.

Spread before us today is the sad record of six thousand years of human experimentation with freedom, ranging from the philosophy of the dictator, who declares that freedom must be defined within the framework of his individual desires, to the philosophy of anarchy, which says that freedom

means the right of every man to do what he pleases when he wants to do it. The Bible, however, very simply defines freedom. It presents God as the rightful Ruler of the universe, whose will described in the Scriptures constitutes the basis for all human thought and behaviour. Man was happiest when he operated within the framework of moral law, because the Creator built him as a moral being. As long as man, by God's power, maintained a healthy relationship with his Maker, all was well. He knew unlimited happiness and endless peace. The Creator never intended that strife, hatred, prejudice, war, sickness, disease, death, and famine should ever invade the universe. Indeed, these things never would have existed had men and angels lived in harmony with the moral law of love.

In Isaiah 14:12-14 we read of an angel who pierced the curtain of universal peace with a statement of selfish purpose: "How art thou fallen from heaven, O Lucifer, son of the morning! how art thou cut down to the ground, which didst weaken the nations! For thou hast said in thine heart, I will ascend into heaven, I will exalt my throne above the stars of God: I will sit also upon the mount of the congregation, in the sides of the north: I will ascend above the heights of the clouds; I will be like the most High."

Restive under God's wise, just, and moral restraints, Lucifer started out on a course of his own by experimenting with a new brand of liberty that would set him free from the moral restraints of the Monarch of the universe. He challenged God's wisdom, love, and authority, thus creating the chaotic state which he transferred to our earth. "And there was war in heaven: Michael and his angels fought against the dragon; and the dragon fought and his angels, and prevailed not; neither was their place found any more in heaven. And the great dragon was cast out, that old serpent, called the Devil, and Satan, which deceiveth the whole world: he was cast out into the earth, and his angels were cast out with him" (Revelation 12:7-9).

Today he tempts man to embark on the same course that he originally took. Adam and Eve, up to the time of the Fall, had been free within the framework of moral law. They observed God's law because they loved and trusted Him. To change this attitude Lucifer had to peck away at their faith in God, which he did with telling effect. He induced our first parents to depart from the path of obedience and to experiment with the "greater freedom," and our eyes can see the sorry record of succeeding generations. Instead of freedom, man now endures slavery both to an alien spiritual power and to his own sinful inclinations.

"And ye shall know the truth, and the truth shall make you free" (John 8:32).

"Sanctify them through thy truth: thy word is truth" (chapter 17:17).

Genuine freedom, then, is possible only within the framework of truth. God's Word safeguards genuine liberty. Genuine freedom is not freedom to do what I want to do, but freedom to do what I ought to do. When we exercise true freedom, we shall not trample upon the rights of others or infringe upon their prerogatives. "O that thou hadst hearkened to my commandments! then had thy peace been as a river, and thy righteousness as the waves of the sea" (Isaiah 48:18). God's law safeguards our tranquillity. When the mind harmonizes with Christ's mind and when man totally agrees with his Maker, the resultant life is that of a free man, for "where the Spirit of the Lord is, there is liberty."

But those who rebel against the moral principles of God's law do not seek liberty, but license. They would declare right and wrong as relative matters and the situation of the moment as a self-justifying entity. The archdeceiver, Lucifer himself, has planned it this way so that he can destroy in man's mind all sense of moral obligation to God and fellowmen. Once he does this, the life of man becomes like a rudderless ship—without discipline, without guidance, and without direction.

While I was standing in an art gallery observing some modern art and not comprehending very well what I saw, a young man walked up to me and said, "The key to understanding modern art is to know that it reflects our time. True art will depict life as it is." That is why some are mystified by the portrayals on a canvas. They do not have this key of understanding.

The artists are correct. These are chaotic times, but man may make this into his finest hour by turning to God with all his heart. Then will the language of the Negro spiritual be fulfilled in him:

"Free at last, free at last,
    I thank God I'm free at last."

Education

"And Jesus answered him, saying, It is written, That man shall not live by bread alone, but by every word of God" (Luke 4:4).

God's Word is the food of the soul. What we put into our bodies will feed our bodies, but only the Word of the living God can build up the spiritual attitude. It is the food by which the soul lives.

The King James Version of the Bible contains 1,189 chapters, 31,-173 verses, and 810,697 words. The Old and New Testaments are divided into sixty-six books. Approximately forty writers wrote the Bible over a period of 1,500 years, and it is remarkable that so many writers, stretched over so long a period of time, could write without contradicting one another. Surely we can regard this as evidence of the divine origin of the Book. "Knowing this first, that no prophecy of the scripture is of any private interpretation. For the prophecy came not in old time by the will of man: but holy men of God spake as they were moved by the Holy Ghost" (2 Peter 1:20, 21).

The Scriptures are historically accurate, prophetically correct, and faithful interpreters of the present. The Bible tells man who he is, where he came from, and where he is going. Here alone may we receive the guidance for living so necessary for the enjoyment of the more abundant life.

"All scripture is given by inspiration of God, and is profitable for doctrine, for reproof, for correction, for instruction in righteousness: that the man of God may be perfect, throughly furnished unto all good works" (2 Timothy 3:16, 17).

Atheists, agnostics, and infidels have risen and hurled their anathemas at this Book, but it has survived them all. It is today the world's best-seller, and yet, somehow, it is the least read—with its principles seldom practiced. However, it is God's Word to man—the verbal revelation of God's will, character, and power. Those who read it become aware of the fact that God

102

One of the leading Black universities has been Howard University in Washington, D.C. DAVID B. SHERWIN loves them with a deep and everlasting love. The whole life of Christ and His dealings with man are verbalized in the Word of God. That is why the Bible declares that men should not live by bread alone but by every word that God speaks. In John 6:63, Jesus said, "The words that I speak unto you, they are spirit, and they are life."

So the words of the living God are the food for the soul. We must look to the Word of God to build up our spiritual bodies into unshakable towers of strength. There can be no genuine emancipation without the keen insights and intelligence afforded from the study of God's Word.

When the black man received his freedom from slavery, a few people understood that if he was ever to be built up into the first-class citizen he was supposed to become, there would have to be established a system of education that would make him literate. They understood that he could not remain in ignorance and enjoy all the privileges of citizenship. So in spite of danger to themselves, many Northern whites journeyed south and established schools, academies, colleges, and seminaries to uplift the black race. General O. O. Howard, head of the Freedmen's Bureau, helped found Howard University in Washington, D.C. Many of today's leading Negro colleges and universities are the product of this new era of education. Some of the schools started during or shortly after Reconstruction were Fisk University, Atlanta University, Hampton Institute, Morgan State College, Tougaloo College in Mississippi, Oakwood College in Alabama, Knoxville College, and Tuskegee Institute.

And so it is in the realm of the

spiritual. We cannot rise from the lowlands of sinful living without the benefits that come from the study of God's Word. Any attempt at spiritual excellence without this vital influence is merely whistling in the dark. The most truly Christian are those who study God's Word, and who, by the help that God gives them, order their lives in harmony with His eternal principles. The study of God's Word sows the seed for the giant oak of spiritual excellence that one day will provide refreshing shade for weary travelers.

While it is true that after slavery many Negroes found themselves without the means to earn a livelihood, it is equally true that thousands of them were artisans and workers in iron before they came to this country. It is said that of the 120,000 artisans in the South at the end of the Civil War, 100,000 were Negroes. They worked as gunsmiths, plasterers, cabinetmakers, blacksmiths, masons, river pilots, and engineers. Men can make it on their own to certain levels of excellence, but add to it the refinement of education, and they soar to lofty heights!

Similarly, in spiritual things men with a limited knowledge of the Scriptures may indeed give evidence of a measure of God's grace within them, but to pursue the Word of God with the passion of a hungry or thirsty man is to find a level of spiritual greatness.

"In the beginning was the Word, and the Word was with God, and the Word was God" (John 1:1).

This passage introduces us to a fresh aspect of the Word of God by using it as one of the names of

Jesus, the Son of the living God. "All things were made by him; and without him was not any thing made that was made. In him was life; and the life was the light of men" (verses 3,4).

Jesus Christ as the Incarnate Word is the Logos of the Scriptures, the Living Word. The Bible is the Written Word, and when it speaks, it speaks about God's character, power, and wisdom. Christ came as the living embodiment of all that the Written Word had said. In this sense He was the fulfillment of the Scriptures. "And the Word was made flesh, and dwelt among us, (and we beheld his glory, the glory as of the only begotten of the Father,) full of grace and truth" (verse 14).

Christ acted out both the spirit and the letter of God's Written Word, and as there is no conflcit in Him, so there is none in His Word. The Old Testament is the New Testament concealed. The New Testament is the Old Testament revealed. Both reveal the character, will, wisdom, and power of the true and living God.

Of the Old Testament, Jesus said in John 5:46,47: "For had ye believed Moses, ye would have believed me: for he wrote of me. But if ye believe not his writings, how shall ye believe my words?" Jesus taught that the Bible is an entity. In its totality it reveals God's love for man. To reject the Old Testament is to misinterpret the New, and to reject the New Testament is to entirely misread the Old.

A mother, wondering at the brilliance of her little boy who was easily putting a jigsaw puzzle together, inquired of him, "Son, why do you find it so easy to put that jigsaw puzzle together?"

Pointing to the other side of the jigsaw puzzle, the little boy put his finger on the figure of a man and indicated that in assembling the puzzle he was following the outline of the man. "There's a man in it," he answered.

This is how we may more completely and thoroughly understand the Bible. There's a man in it, the man Christ Jesus. "Search the Scriptures; for in them ye think ye have eternal life: and they are they which testify of me" (chapter 5:39). When we recognize the Man in them and who He is, they make sense whether they be the Old Testament Scriptures or the New.

Jesus makes obedience to His Word a condition for a continued relationship with Him. In Luke 6:46 we read, "And why call ye me, Lord, Lord, and do not the things which I say?" In our prayers we call upon the name of the Lord, but He makes it clear that He will not hear our prayers if we bypass His Word in seeking to establish a relationship with Him. "Don't even call My name," says Jesus, "unless you respect My Word." But how many thousands walk past that Book every day as they busily seek to earn a living. Going about the mundane affairs of day-to-day existence, they bypass the source of divine power right at their fingertips.

A song says, "There is dust on the Bible, dust on the Holy Word." Apart from this Book, we cannot know that God has delivered us.

It is said that after the issuance of the Emancipation Proclamation many slaves continued in slavery unaware of their freedom. Others knew they were free, but because of the insecurity of facing the future, they turned back to bondage. Yet others hired themselves out as tenant farmers for the security of a shack to sleep in and food to eat. Thus tied to the land, they worked themselves into a debt from which they could not extricate themselves, thus reenslaving themselves while legally free.

Likewise many men and women who are enslaved to habits that damage the soul and destroy the spiritual nature do not know that nineteen hundred years ago at Calvary their emancipation document was signed with the blood of the Lamb of God. Others who are vaguely aware of this fact neglect reading the Scriptures, and thus lose their sense of the truthfulness of the gospel message and, though legally free, reenslave themselves.

However, some blacks, like Booker T. Washington, thirsted so deeply for knowledge that they worked their way through those primitive colleges with a broom and the sweat of their brow until they had educated themselves and emerged as servants who helped uplift their own people. George Washington Carver, sold for a racehorse, later climbed to such eminence that the United States Congress, in session, sat in rapt attention as he revealed the mysteries of nature that were his subject of research.

So should it be with us as we seek to excel spiritually. Our hunger must be so intense and our thirst so strong that nothing less than a thorough knowlidge of God's will as found in His Word will satisfy us.

The Bottom Line

When someone talks of the "nitty-gritty," he is speaking of the heart of the matter. If he has penetrated through the form to the substance, he is now prepared to talk about things as they really are. In hard bargaining it means that you are now prepared to talk terms and to come to grips with reality—probably the most difficult thing for a man to do. We spend large portions of our lives dealing with peripheral matters and waste our vital substance on nonessentials. It would be shocking, indeed, if we could make a record of the years spent on that which is truly substantial along with those years wasted on less meaningful projects. Even in our common understanding we do not usually penetrate to the heart of the matter.

Let us consider the question of sin in the light of this. What is it? We commonly understand it to be breaking God's rules, and that is true. "Sin is the transgression of the law" (1 John 3:4). But sin is more than breaking rules, for at Calvary sin broke God's heart. Let us then penetrate to the true nature of this spiritual disease, and perhaps in discovering its nature, we can find a cure.

God's written rules have grown out of His character. They express His state of mind and nature. They tell us who God is and how He thinks. In short, the rules define the terms of our moral relationship with Him. Viewed in this light, then, sin destroys that relationship by alienating man from his Maker. "Thou hast wearied me with thine iniquities" (Isaiah 43:24). "And when ye spread forth your hands, I will hide mine eyes from you: yea, when ye make many prayers, I will not hear: your hands are full of blood" (chapter 1:15).

Sin, therefore, is a bit more serious than merely breaking rules. It is alienation from God. It breaks that essential fellowship between the creature and the Creator, and this is serious because the creature cannot live fully without the Creator. Transgression tarnishes

Scripture reveals our salvation. MEYLAN THORESEN

those things that are truly meaningful to life. This we must understand, and that is why tampering with sin is so dangerous. Sin grieves God. "Grieve not the holy Spirit of God, whereby ye are sealed unto the day of redemption" (Ephesians 4:30). Sin in its strictest sense violates the terms of man's relationship with his Maker, and therefore results in separation from God, which leads

to spiritual death. Understandably, then, Christ said to Nicodemus, "Marvel not that I said unto thee, ye must be born again" (John 3:7). The living dead must be born again in order to live again. This is the heart of the matter.

But what about salvation? It is a salvage operation. If you were to visit one of the large automobile graveyards that bedeck many of our highways, you would find that occasionally a truck will load on a few of these old hacks and take them to a refinery, where the metal is resmelted. It then reappears as new automobiles, refrigerators, and other serviceable utensils. A useful and meaningful transformation occurs under the fires of the great refineries. This is what Christ does for the sinner. He covers him with His blood and cleanses him by His grace, and he becomes a new creature in Christ.

But how can Christ do this? By an act of justification. In its primary sense justification is a judicial act, for man cannot be restored to fellowship with God except by an act of God. Romans 7:18 clearly states man's inability to better himself and to change his status: "For I know that in me (that is, in my flesh,) dwelleth no good thing: for to will is present with me; but how to perform that which is good I find not." And in the following verse he adds, "For the good that I would I do not: but the evil which I would not, that I do." Having alienated ourselves from God by surrendering either to our own sinful nature or to environmental pressures, we have but one hope for recovery—that Someone outside of us and above us, namely, the Creator Himself, declare us once again members of the heavenly family. By His grace God effects this change in status, and He bases it on Christ's merit alone. We receive justification by faith in Christ.

When we accept Him as our Saviour, He performs this righteous act of grace for us. We are then no longer sons and daughters of the evil one, but once again sons and daughters of God. "Therefore being justified by faith, we have peace with God through our Lord Jesus Christ" (Romans 5:1). Once this becomes our experience, we can rest our minds over our past transgressions. "I have blotted out, as a thick cloud, thy transgressions, and, as a cloud, thy sins: return unto me; for I have redeemed thee. Sing, O ye heavens; for the Lord hath done it: shout, ye lower parts of the earth: break forth into singing, ye mountains, O forest, and every tree therein: for the Lord hath redeemed Jacob, and glorified himself in Israel" (Isaiah 44:22,23).

Redemption changes our status before God and makes a noticeable difference in our relationship to our fellowman. "Jesus answered, Verily, verily, I say unto thee, Except a man be born of water and of the Spirit, he cannot enter into the kingdom of God. That which is born of the flesh is flesh; and that which is born of the Spirit is spirit. Marvel not that I said unto thee, ye must be born again" (John 3:5-7). When a man is born of the Spirit, a change occurs in his thoughts, words, and deeds. "For every one that doeth evil hateth the light, neither cometh to the light, lest his deeds should be reproved. But he that doeth truth cometh to the light, that his deeds may be made manifest, that they are wrought in God" (verses 20, 21).

The early portions of the third chapter of John speak of the work of God in behalf of man and within the human experience. The latter part of the chapter reveals the fruits of this internal operation. Our deeds must change so that they will bear the close scrutiny of God. Dark deeds have no place in the experience of the born-again child of God.

Now, what about translation? This old world has already been condemned. After thousands of years of transgression, how could it possibly survive? Even thinking men of nonclerical professions sometimes give this world only five to ten years before it is consumed in the horror of the mushroom cloud. The Bible, however, correctly describes the future of the world. "Behold, the Lord maketh the earth empty, and maketh it waste, and turneth it upside down, and scattereth abroad the inhabitants thereof" (Isaiah 24:1). Verse 20 says, "The earth shall reel to and fro like a drunkard, and shall be removed like a cottage; and the transgression thereof shall be heavy upon it; and it shall fall, and not rise again." In view of this coming calamity, obviously God's people will have to go somewhere. God will literally transplant or translate them to another world; the Bible assures us that He will do this. "Let not your heart be troubled: ye believe in God, believe also in me. In my Father's house are many mansions: if it were not so, I would have told you. I go to prepare a place for you. And if I go and prepare a place for you, I will come again, and receive you unto myself; that where I am, there ye may be also" (John 14:1-3).

Christ will rescue his believing children. He assures all who turn to Him in faith that He will not leave them on this earth during the coming calamity. "And I looked, and, lo, a Lamb stood on the mount Sion, and with him an hundred forty and four thousand, having his Father's name written in their foreheads. And I heard a voice from heaven, as the voice of many waters, and as the voice of a great thunder: and I heard the voice of harpers harping with their harps: and they sung as it were a new song before the throne, and before the four beasts, and the elders: and no man could learn that song but the hundred and forty and four thousand, which were redeemed from the earth. These are they which were not defiled with women; for they are virgins. These are they which follow the Lamb whithersoever he goeth. These were redeemed from among men, being the firstfruits unto God and to the Lamb" (Revelation 14:1-4).

The Christian may, indeed, look forward unashamedly to a better world. Some deride the Christian for his emphasis on the kingdom of God. They would focus all on the here and now, but the Christian knows better than this. He knows that while he must live and serve now, giving himself totally and completely to the betterment of humanity and God's service, this world, in effect, already stands condemned. If there is no other world, then Christians are of all men most miserable, and their lives are hopeless. And so our vision of the world to come inspires us to greater activity here. Our knowledge that God has prepared a city for the saints inspires us both to endure and to work away at the problems that now plague the human family. It may not then be truthfully said that religion is the opiate of the people. Sin is the opiate of the people. The religion of Jesus Christ makes us alive.

Before I'd Be
a Slave

According to the Bible, the human family is one, having proceeded from a common source, and will share a common destiny. "And Adam called his wife's name Eve; because she was the mother of all living" (Genesis 3:20). From this pair came the entire human family. A few years later, when the God of heaven flooded the earth, only eight persons survived. All men and women living have descended from those survivors. After a few years had passed and the sons of men began to spread over the earth, the Lord Himself said, "Behold, the people is one, and they all have one language; and this they begin to do: and now nothing will be restrained from them, which they have imagined to do" (chapter 11:6).

Notice the two important points: (1) the human family is one; (2) they all speak one language. Clearly at this point of human history, there were no divergent races of people springing from different sources. Genesis 11 describes them as one great big family, and from them came all of the inhabitants of the earth. "So the Lord scattered them abroad from thence upon the face of all the earth: and they left off to build the city. Therefore is the name of it called Babel; because the Lord did there confound the language of all the earth: and from thence did the Lord scatter them abroad upon the face of all the earth" (verses 8, 9).

Ham, Shem, and Japheth, Noah's sons, survived the great floodwaters that had ravaged the earth. From them came the great conglomerate family that spoke one language and that built the great Tower of Babel. God turned His attention to this group and confused their language. They then scattered over the face of the earth.

We should notice at this point that all were members of one family, and they developed their indigenous characteristics by inbreeding in varying climates and under different working conditions. Under these circumstances, differing cultural practices, skin pigmentations, and hair textures would develop. None of this, however, could destroy the fact of interracial kinship. Basically all human beings are brothers. "Have we not all one father? hath not one God created us? why do we deal treacherously every man against his brother, by profaning the covenant of our fathers?" (Malachi 2:10). The apostle Paul, under differing circumstances, thunders this same momumental truth: "And hath made of one blood all nations of men for to dwell on all the face of the earth, and hath determined the times before appointed, and the bounds of their habitation" (Acts 17:26).

Why then is there treachery between brothers? Why do men enslave their fellowmen, segregate them, mistreat them, and do them harm? Why does brother fight brother on the world's battlefields? Someone has said, "Man has learned to fly the air like a bird, to swim the sea like a fish, but when will he learn to walk the earth like a brother?"

The world, because of increased and more efficient communications, has shrunk to a neighborhood. Never was it more dangerous than it is today for schisms to develop between nations and the races of people. Man might well devote 90 percent of his energies to studying ways and means of living harmoniously with his brother. Benjamin Franklin once said, "We must all hang together, or assuredly we shall all hang separately."

A man cannot really have a right relationship with his brother if he lives out of harmony with his heavenly Father. The whole concept of the brotherhood of man is based on the Biblical teaching of the Fatherhood of God. Our primary responsibility, then, is to develop a correct relationship with our Creator. Only this will enable us to relate properly to those with whom we live and work every day. "If a man say, I love God, and hateth his brother, he is a liar: for he that loveth not his brother whom he hath seen, how can he love God whom he hath not seen? And this commandment have we from him, That he who loveth God love his brother also" (1 John 4:20, 21).

It is sheer hypocrisy to claim to love God while we despise our fellowman, and yet thousands give money for the conversion of people overseas, but when they meet these same individuals face to face, they are so uncomfortable and embarrassed that they do not treat them civilly. Such persons need the new birth. Divine love has not properly conditioned their hearts to exercise brotherly love. Here lies the root of our international problems. The world seeks to harmonize the nations without any reference to God, but it is only when we are right with God that we can be right with each other. Furthermore, we cannot be right with God and at odds with each other. The same gospel that reconciles man and God also reconciles man and man. When the love of God truly possesses the heart, such superficialities as skin pigmentation or national origin fade into insignificance in the face of the broader claims of divine love implanted in the human heart. The truly free are those who truly love.

The apostle Peter lived at a time

Astronaut Guion S. Bluford, during his mission in space, could look down and see that humanity shares but one world. NASA

TE-8

when the common consensus among Jews was that all non-Jews were unclean and unworthy of social acceptance. He had to discover for himself that this was not true. When he did, he confessed, "Ye know how that it is an unlawful thing for a man that is a Jew to keep company, or come unto one of another nation; but God hath shewed me that I should not call any man common or unclean" (Acts 10:28). The refining fires of divine love completely demolish the caste system along with all its related evil.

Since the arrival of numerous black men on these shores, the problem of applying the Biblical principles of human brotherhood has plagued this nation. The black man was regarded as mere chattel property and not as a human being, and thus treated as such. In those early years, professed Christians would permit a slave to worship in the same building with them but only in a "buzzard's roost" reserved for those of "lower caste." The pulpit subjected these slaves to such teachings as "Obey your masters." Some men of religion went so far as to try to justify slavery on Biblical grounds by artfully twisting scriptures out of their historical and logical contexts. These became the most popular preachers in the Southern white community.

In all fairness I should also point out that the clergy in the North generally exhibited little or no concern over slavery and its terrible effects upon both the slave and the slave owner. Several notable exceptions deserve our tribute, though, for in those days even the North harbored such proslavery sentiment that a minister preaching against the evils of slavery would likely be tarred and feathered and ridden out of town on a rail.

The Northern interest in slavery, however, differed from that of the South. Northerners looked to the South as a profitable marketplace, and frowned upon anything that would upset this market. Nevertheless, powerful preachers such as Henry Ward Beecher and Theodore Parker joined Wendel Phillips and William Lloyd Garrison in thundering against this malignant evil. Also at this time the pen of a frail woman, Ellen G. White, traced the bitterest denunciation of slavery that has yet come to this author's attention. She rebuked it as an evil unparalleled in the history of the world even in heathen lands.

The sledgehammer blows lev-

eled against slavery by civil and religious leaders precipitated the Civil War and the final determination of the slavery question. But how would the nation deal with its newly freed minority? Would the Christian principles of human brotherhood apply here? What alternatives did the government face? Since relatively few black men lived on this continent then, even Abraham Lincoln considered deporting the black man to Africa. But the black man had been on this continent as long as the white man had. He had accompanied such explorers as Columbus and Balboa. The black man's toil had formed the very basis of this nation's early economy. Deportation would only avert making a Christian decision.

Then Abraham Lincoln was assassinated, and Thaddeus Stevens, of Pennsylvania, championed the passage of the Thirteenth and Fourteenth Amendments to the Constitution, which guaranteed that the nation would integrate the black man into American society. But another decision yet remains unresolved: Will the Negro be so economically and socially assimilated into American society that he will eventually lose his identity through intermarriage and general assimilation? Or will he, like the Hebrews before him, resort to community action based on the present ghetto structure and assume control of the economic life within the ghetto, while integrating institutions outside of the ghettos that may be meaningful to his progress and prosperity? Or will a system of apartheid confine the black man to large, government-supported reservations, where he will have inter-

nal autonomy while ruled by a national government, yet remain separated in deed and in fact from the mainstream of national life? Or, as some groups suggest, will he be allocated certain States where he could function on this continent as a separate government entirely?

Since in the American population the Negro numbers one in twelve, it appears unlikely that a fifth alternative, that of armed revolt against the government, would succeed, although sizable numbers of revolutionaries conceivably could create havoc in our country and could leave nothing surviving that would be meaningful to anyone. Therefore, rational men must, in all honesty, discount the fifth proposition.

Also certain evidence indicates that black people would generally give little support to the scheme to rope off certain States and allow a separate black government to function within the framework of a white government. As the matter stands now, black men also show little enthusiasm for a program of total assimilation in which their identity would disappear in intermarriage. When the black man talks about integration, he does not mean this at all. He has no more desire to lose his significance as a black man in American society than does anyone else.

When the black man speaks of integration, he means equality of opportunity that relates to every meaningful aspect of American life. This is what the blackman wants. He is no more or less interested in social mingling than is his white brother. Historically, of course, some social mingling has gone on

Earthquakes, such as this one in Mexico City, signal the Lord's return. UPI/BETTMANN
NEWSPHOTOS

and probably always will.

It seems that the present consensus among black people is that full and complete equality of opportunity be granted them as citizens now. Let every organization and service that is meaningful to any citizen be made available to all citizens here and now. We must relegate the old concept of the "slow process of evolution" to the scrap heap and understand it for what it is, namely, a stalling device. Would it be selfishness to deny others opportunities available to ourselves? While black men desire the day when their white brothers will regard them as human beings regardless of their skin pigmentation and hair texture, they are more interested in their children going to the best schools, getting the best training, and living the best lives than they are in being invited to the Christmas or Thanksgiving dinner. Black people, generally, are less interested in sitting beside white people or conversing with them or being invited to their social affairs than they are in being able to buy decent housing wherever it is if they can afford it.

It seems at this point that the future of the black man lies in controlling his own social and economic affairs within the large ghetto areas while he integrates all organizations and services that are meaningful to all men outside of the ghetto areas. To the black man integration does not mean being stripped of his identity and being treated as if he were not black. He wants others to deal with him as a human being that is black. This seems to be the way of the future, and I would like to suggest a Christian solution for what has historically proved a very knotty problem.

Whites who would risk all to preserve the status quo and blacks who would destroy the nation to achieve their ends both stand repudiated not only by divine principle but by the collective disapproval of the vast majority of Americans. We must remember that no revolution has completely succeeded in history. All have either overshot or undershot their mark. Therefore, we must view the future through the eyes of God's prophets for a clear understandng of what the future holds for all people, and thus temper out aspirations and efforts with the sure knowledge that comes from a study of the future through God's Word.

And what does the Bible say of the future? It says that all human governments must ultimately fail, for they are founded upon the shifting sands of human weakness. "And there were voices, and thunders, and lightnings; and there was a great earthquake, such as was not since men were upon the earth, so mighty an earthquake, and so great. And the great city was divided into three parts, and the cities of the nations fell: and great Babylon came in remembrance before God, to give unto her the cup of the wine of the fierceness of his wrath. And every island fled away, and the mountains were not found" (Revelation 16:18-20). "Behold, I come as a thief. Blessed is he that watcheth, and keepeth his garments, lest he walk naked, and they see his shame" (verse 15).

We must, therefore, conclude that while we work in Christ's spirit of love for human justice, we must understand that ultimately only frustration will come to any human government, for men separated from God are basically unjust. Out

of the selfishness of their human hearts they will, whether black, white, red, or yellow, heap upon their less-fortunate fellowmen the fruits of prejudice and pride—segregation, discrimination, and human bondage.

Revival may succeed, where revolution cannot. The French revolution toppled the monarch but produced a Napoleon, who became the scourge of Europe until at last he was exiled to the island of St. Helena. No war ever accomplished its purpose. World War I toppled the kaiser, but it produced a Hitler, who subjected the world to a man-made hell, from which it has not yet recovered.

Do not place too much faith in anything that man constructs. Instead, build your house of faith upon the Rock, Christ Jesus, so that when the storms of life beat upon it in their fury, your house will stand. We should remind ourselves that our emancipation was not accomplished without God. From the slave plantations voices ascended to heaven pleading for deliverance from the hand of the oppressor.

During more recent years, under the leadership of Martin Luther King, Jr., the church constituted the center of commitment and the source of fortitude that carried the protest movement to one success after another. In this hour of crisis, may we remember Christ, who made possible Israel's exodus from Egypt. Unfortunately, when Israel entered the land of Canaan, they took up the idolatry of the land, had their strength and morality sapped, and were finally dispersed among the nations. May we profit from their mistakes.

The Queen of Sheba

"Princes shall come out of Egypt; Ethiopia shall soon stretch out her hands unto God" (Psalm 68:31). This text has been used by many to fire the Negroes' dreams of a day of future temporal greatness when a black kingdom would one day rule the world.

This view of the Scriptures could be misleading and as disastrous as was the ancient Jewish interpretation of the Messianic prophecies. As you know, the rabbis interpreted the Messianic prophecies to mean that the Messiah would establish an earthly kingdom in which the Jews would control the world. Hence, they were quite unprepared for the Messiah when He came that evening in Bethlehem of Judea as a baby born to Mary. Wise men from a far-off land had correctly interpreted the prophecies and stood ready to acclaim Him King, but the established Jewish rulers and rabbis did not notice this grand event. Not even during the disciples' three and a half years of association with Christ did they understand the nature of the kingdom he had come to establish. And when they saw him suffer, bleed, and die at Calvary, their hopes were crushed as all of their dreams tumbled to the earth.

It is positively dangerous to misinterpret a prophecy of the Scriptures, arousing hopes that are destined to fail. This could lead to frustration and erratic action that could bring upon the head of the whole race the wrath of the majority. This, in turn, would surely mean the destruction of this country. Let us study, therefore, the future course of world events and discover, if possible, the true meaning of the text "Ethiopia shall soon stretch out her hands unto God."

In the second chapter of the book of Daniel, we have the story of ancient Babylon's King Nebuchadnezzar, who had a dream which he forgot upon awakening. According to the Scriptures, he called in his magicians and fortune-tellers and asked them not only to give him the meaning of the dream but to recall the dream itself. After a hurried consultation, "the Chaldeans answered before the king, and said, There is not a man upon the earth that can shew the king's matter: therefore there is no king, lord, nor ruler, that asked such things at any magician, or astrologer, or Chaldean. And it is a rare thing that the king requireth, and there is none other that can shew it before the king, except the gods, whose dwelling is not with flesh" (verses 10, 11). Their answer infuriated the king, and he ordered the death of all the wise men.

Now Daniel happened to be a wise man in the Babylonian kingdom, and he, with three of his companions, requested a stay of the king's order so that they might pray to the God of heaven, who alone could reveal the answer to the king's dilemma. King Nebuchadnezzar granted their request, and after praying, "then was the secret revealed unto Daniel in a night vision. Then Daniel blessed the God of heaven" (verse 19). Later Daniel appeared before the king and revealed to the astonished ruler not only the dream but its interpretation also.

Daniel carefully gave credit where credit was due. He said, "There is a God in heaven that revealeth secrets, and maketh known to the king Nebuchadnezzar what shall be in the latter days. Thy dream, and the visions of thy head upon thy bed, are these" (verse 28). He said that the king had seen an image of a man in his dream. The image's head was of gold, the breast and arms of silver, the stomach and thighs of brass, the legs of iron, and the feet a mixture of iron

119

and clay. Then a large stone broke loose and struck the image on the feet, grinding the whole image to powder. The stone then grew until it became a great mountain filling the whole earth.

Daniel's interpretation of the dream is important to us because it actually spells out the future of the world from Nebuchadnezzar's day right down to the end of all human civilization. In verses 38 and 39 Daniel said to the monarch, "Thou art this head of gold. And after thee shall arise another kingdom inferior to thee." Medo-Persia conquered Babylon and ruled the world from 539 to 331 B.C. Next came the Kingdom of Grecia, the brass kingdom referred to in verse 39. It ruled from 331 to 168 B.C. In verse 40 Daniel predicted that the fourth kingdom would be as strong as iron, referring to none other than the iron monarchy of Rome, which ruled from 168 B.C. to A.D. 476. Then according to Daniel, no world empire would follow Rome, but world history would be a matter of fragmented kingdoms.

"And whereas thou sawest iron mixed with miry clay, they shall mingle themselves with the seed of men: but they shall not cleave one to another, even as iron is not mixed with clay" (verse 43). Daniel predicted that men would even try intermarriage between heads of state, but nothing would again unite the world under one empire as had been the case under Babylon, Medo-Persia, Greece, and Rome. And further, in verse 42, Daniel predicted that some nations would be strong and some weak. "As the toes of the feet were part of iron, and part of clay, so the king-

dom shall be partly strong, and partly broken." A look at the map of the world today clearly indicates how accurately the prophet predicted our day. America, Russia, France, and Britain have the atomic bomb and are economically strong. Yet many other nations are truly as weak as clay.

Clearly we are living in the very toes of the statue that Nebuchadnezzar saw in his dream some 2,500 years ago. In our own day men have defied the power of Bible prophecy and sought to break the truthfulness of Daniel's prediction. They have tried to unite the nations under one head, but all have failed. Charlemagne, Kaiser Wilhelm, Napoleon Bonaparte, and Adolf Hitler have gone the way of all flesh. They have butted their heads against the divine prophecies and have lost.

The Word of God cannot fail. "Heaven and earth shall pass away, but my words shall not pass away" (Matthew 24:35). But Daniel continues, "And in the days of these kings shall the God of heaven set up a kingdom, which shall never be destroyed: and the kingdom shall not be left to other people, but it shall break in pieces and consume all these kingdoms, and it shall stand for ever" (Daniel 2:44).

This is the prediction of Christ's second coming. Nineteen hundred years ago He said, "Let not your heart be troubled: ye believe in God, believe also in me. In my Father's house are many mansions: if it were not so, I would have told you. I go to prepare a place for you. And if I go and prepare a place for you, I will come again, and receive you unto myself; that where I am, there ye may be also" (John 14:1-3). Christ will come back to this earth, and He will eventually set up a kingdom here that He Himself will rule. It "shall not be left to other people," the Bible says. At no point in the history of civilization do the Scriptures record that the black races will once again rule the world.

But what does our text mean? I believe that a revival of godliness will spring up among black people around the world. I believe that Ethiopia shall yet stretch forth her hands to God.

Coptic literature relates that a queen of Sheba who visited Jerusalem during the reign of King Solomon was from Ethiopia. The Bible says that Solomon told her everything her heart desired, which means that most likely he introduced her to the worship of the true God. Coptic tradition holds that the Queen of Sheba carried this information back to Ethiopia.

In our own century, we have witnessed a resurgence of revival among black people. In Africa the gospel is going by leaps and bounds. Thousands of adherents are being converted to Christ yearly, and in North America there is a great turning to God on the part of black people. Black men everywhere look to Heaven for deliverance. Expectantly they scan the sky for our Lord's appearance. Black preachers crisscross the earth with the message of the nearness of His return.

Human civilization has had its day. Soon the time will come when the skyscrapers built by human hands will fall into masses of rubble and twisted steel under the sledgehammer blows of avenging God. Christ has been ignored. He has been ruled out of His own universe. He has been denied. And an insulted Creator will return to this earth to give to every man a reward according to how he accepted or rejected Christ. Are you ready for that day? This is the day when Ethiopia must stretch forth her hands to God. If not now, when? If not here, where? If not we, who?

Thy Kingdom Come

"For even hereunto were ye called: because Christ also suffered for us, leaving us an example, that ye should follow his steps: who did no sin, neither was guile found in his mouth: who, when he was reviled, reviled not again; when he suffered, he threatened not; but committed himself to him that judgeth righteously" (1 Peter 2:21-23).

Peter's statement embodies the Christian philosophy on nonviolence, the highest point of Christian excellence and the goal of the soul. It is the exact opposite of human nature, which, when threatened, is tempted to threaten back, or if reviled, reviles again. In the language of the streets, "We like to give tit for tat." A philosophy of reciprocity is the principle of carnal human nature. Even little boys when sat upon by others are expected to fight their way out of it, returning blow for blow and conquering by force if possible. The philosophy of this world is that might makes right. It is only the strong and aggressive that are the fittest, and they alone will survive.

However, Jesus stated the basis for nonviolent reaction to oppression. "My kingdom is not of this world: if my kingdom were of this world, then would my servants fight, that I should not be delivered to the Jews: but now is my kingdom not from hence" (John 18:36). Jesus disclaims all responsibility for the mistake-prone civilizations that man has created under the influence of an alien power. There are evils in society which we can and must eradicate, but the Christian must fight them nonviolently, using spiritual weapons, for this present civilization faces destruction at the hands of God. "Behold, the Lord maketh the earth empty, and maketh it waste, and turneth it upside down, and scattereth abroad the inhabitants thereof. . . . The land shall be utterly emptied, and utterly spoiled: for the Lord hath spoken this word" (Isaiah 24:1, 3). The prophet Peter predicts, "The day of the Lord will come as a thief in the night; in the

All races will live together in God's kingdom.

which the heavens shall pass away with a great noise, and the elements shall melt with fervent heat, the earth also and the works that are therein shall be burned up" (2 Peter 3:10).

Since God is one day going to burn this faulty, man-created system to the ground and reduce it to ashes, man need not bring guilt upon his own head for doing the same. God looks upon all arson alike, whether performed by an individual or by invading armies or marauding guerrillas. It involves a man taking into his own hands that which God Himself will do—and do more thoroughly than any human being ever could. He will one day eradicate by fire all evil, all injustice, all slum housing, all that man has built. "For, behold, the day cometh, that shall burn as an oven; and all the proud, yea, and all that do wickedly, shall be stubble: and the day that cometh shall burn them up, saith the Lord of hosts, that it shall leave them neither root nor branch" (Malachi 4:1).

The Christian is in the minority because human transgression has corrupted this planet, making him an alien. Throughout history this has been true, for the apostle Paul wrote, "These all died in faith, not having received the promises, but having seen them afar off, and were persuaded of them, and embraced them, and confessed that they were strangers and pilgrims on the earth" (Hebrews 11:13). The Christian, then, does not look for a millennial utopia under a man-created sinless society. He knows that the best he can do on this earth is to better conditions on a limited basis. He knows that inevitably the end of all human civilization must come by a direct act of God. "For the Lord himself shall descend from heaven with a shout, with the voice of the archangel, and with the trump of God: and the dead in Christ shall rise first: then we which are alive and remain shall be caught up together with them in the clouds, to meet the Lord in the air: and so shall we ever be with the Lord" (1 Thessalonians 4:16, 17).

The Lord will return to this earth with cataclysmic power. He will shake the whole earth, and all who have rebelled against his will, will flee from His presence. "And the heaven departed as a scroll when it is rolled together; and every mountain and island were moved out of their places. And the kings of the earth, and the great men, and the rich men, and the chief captains, and the mighty men, and every bondman, and every free man, hid themselves in the dens and in the rocks of the mountains; and said to the mountains and rocks, Fall on us, and hide us from the face of him that sitteth on the throne, and from the wrath of the Lamb: for the great day of his wrath is come; and who shall be able to stand?" (Revelation 6:14-17).

So the Christian's nonviolent posture in this world is rooted in the fact that Christ Himself will even all old scores, forcefully put down the enemies of righteousness, and ultimately exalt His people to positions of prominence and influence on this very planet. The Christian, therefore, works with the fervor of an optimist to improve this present world, although he knows in his innermost soul that only an act of God can straighten it out. His hope in the Lord's coming fires him with fervor to correct those evils that can be corrected here and now. The Christian loves both God and his fellowman, but he is not lulled to sleep by the spasmodic responses of society to the Christian ideal. He does not optimistically look for man to permanently right himself and turn this planet into a restored paradise.

Men who have engaged in civil rights work, hoping to create the kingdom of God on earth through social reform, have, at one time or another, come to this point of frustration and have seen all the labors of their lives crumble in ruins. They had expected too much of human nature. Men have sought to set up the kingdom of God on earth long before our day, only to see it fail as some new dictator assumed powers of life and death and brought down their dreams with a resounding crash.

Jesus taught His disciples that the only way they could fight oppression and evil and at the same time maintain their Christian posture would be through nonviolence, and He demonstrated this in His own life. "He was wounded for our transgressions and bruised for our iniquities," but the total amount of soul force that He brought to bear on the wicked practices of man made its impact on society for time and eternity. He built a kingdom not by a sword but by unselfish love. Today this mysterious Galilean numbers His adherents on every continent and island. They would rather die than bring shame on His spotless name.

Said Jesus, "But I say unto you, Love your enemies, bless them that curse you, do good to them that hate you, and pray for them which despitefully use you, and persecute you; that ye may be the childen of your Father which is in heaven: for he maketh his sun to rise on the evil and on the good, and sendeth rain on the just and on the unjust. For if ye love them which love you, what reward have ye? do not even the publicans the same? And if ye salute your brethren only, what do ye more than others? do not even the publicans so?" (Matthew 5:44-47).

Christ's words sound strange to human ears, to men who rely on hydrogen weapons to balance the peace, to nations who are arming to the teeth for struggles they hope will not come. Hence, Scripture describes the Christian as a pilgrim and a stranger in this world. Since this world is doomed, the Christian's hope is a better world than this. Because our Master's kingdom is not of this world, we must do violence to no man, whatever the issue, however just the cause, for "he that killeth with the sword must be killed with the sword" (Revelation 13:10).

Martin Luther King, Jr., and his aides changed this nation. UPI/BETTMANN NEWSPHOTOS

Our Master enjoins us, "Blessed are ye, when men shall hate you, and when they shall separate you from their company, and shall reproach you, and cast out your name as evil, for the Son of man's sake. Rejoice ye in that day, and leap for joy: for, behold, your reward is great in heaven: for in the like manner did their fathers unto the prophets" (Luke 6:22, 23).

Such patient endurance requires a miracle of divine grace on the human heart. We cannot live like this unless we genuinely love God and our fellowman. "Let this mind be in you, which was also in Christ Jesus" (Philippians 2:5). When converted and transformed by the saving grace of the Lord Jesus, we no longer react as we naturally would.

It is important that the millions of black people in North America, America's largest minority, understand and accept this divine principle, for America stands at a crucial threshold in the development of human relations. It is true that provocations have been many and grievous, and the 350-year history of the black man in America is studded with just cause for meeting fire with fire and sword with sword. Nevertheless, resorting to force and the use of arms to further emancipate the race is sheerest folly. If pursued, it can only bring down on the nation total ruin for everybody.

Those who say, "Let's ruin it for whitey," do not offer me enough argument, for they are also saying, "Let us destroy it for blacks, reds, and yellows as well as whites." Despite segregation laws and the intolerance of some whites, the black man has become so intertwined with the destiny of the nation that whites cannot oppress him without restricting themselves, and they cannot destroy him without destroying themselves.

The man who most clearly enunciated this principle was brutally shot to death on Thursday, April 4, 1968. Evidence seems to indicate that in the closing days of his ministry, he came to realize the impossibility of accomplishing his dream by human efforts. He came to see that segregation, while conquerable by law, was still deeply embedded within millions of human hearts. He saw that it had been so woven into the fabric of American life that, even after laws declared it unconstitutional, there were so many methods of evasion that it would take years to eradicate this malignancy. After a brilliant twelve years of social ministry— which so altered the fabric of national policy that it might be safely said, "After Martin Luther King, Jr., the nation would never be the same again," this gallant warrior laid down his life at the hands of an assassin.

But Martin Luther King, Jr., died knowing that he had made life more worth living for millions of people, black and white, and in his last public utterance he said, "Like anybody, I would like to live a long life. Longevity has its place. But I'm not concerned about that now. I just want to do God's will. And He's allowed me to go up to the mountain. And I've looked over and seen the Promised Land. So I'm happy tonight. I'm not fearing any man. Mine eyes have seen the glory of the coming of the Lord."

Is it possible he understood that this generation or any other would not reach the promised land—that human injustice would drag on until "the kingdoms of this world are become the kingdoms of our Lord, and of his Christ" (Revelation 11:15)? Significantly, he did not complete his statement. What did he really see that night? The fulfillment of Scripture? Only the coming of Christ, the King of kings and Lord of lords, can make truth run down like water and righteousness like a mighty stream. May every valley be exalted and every mountain and hill made low, the crooked places straight and the rough places plain, and may the glory of the Lord be revealed and all flesh see it together. (See Isaiah 40: 4, 5.)

Let us work, then, as if the elimination of human injustice depended upon us, yet knowing that only when Christ comes will the oppressed peoples of all the earth overcome someday.

The opportunities facing the young Black man or woman are unlimited today.

Immovable Object

The Negro spiritual "O Mary, Don't You Weep" celebrates the drowning of Pharaoh's army. The children of Israel had just crossed the Red Sea on dry ground. The waters had come thunderously together, drowning their pursuers and slave owners in the bottom of the sea. Hence, the spiritual triumphantly celebrates the miraculous delivery of Israel from Egyptian bondage, the drowning of the armies of the enslavers, and the removal forever of the threat of reenslavement.

The song addresses Mary, a name picked without reference to the situation at hand. She is told not to weep, that it is a time of rejoicing, that the enslavement of Israel is past, and that a new era of opportunity now lies before her. "O Mary, don't you weep." Thus the black man fired his own hopes for ultimate deliverance. Aware of the totality of his enslavement, he could only hope for some miraculous intervention that would set him free. Then for him also there would be a day of rejoicing as the long road of opportunity, unhindered by slavery, would stretch before him. "O Mary, don't you weep."

The black man sees in the signing of the Emancipation Proclamation and in the outcome of the Civil War a parting of the waters, the beginning of a new life of freedom and dignity for him. Understandably, he does not share the joy and the nostalgia of the slavery years in America. He does not look back but ahead. He has crossed his Jordan. He now moves toward the "Canaan Land" of full citizenship and privilege in this land of opportunity. Against this background, we can well understand the song's counsel to Mary, "Don't you weep."

For the church of the living God, however, the day of weeping is not over. Ever since Cain killed Abel, doers of God's will have been under extreme pressure from their worldly environment. Christianity runs counter to the philosophy which governs this world. It is incompatible with today's state of society. Christ and the world just do not go in the same direction, hence the injunction in 1 John 2:15, "Love not the world, neither the things that are in the world. If any man love the world, the love of the Father is not in him." "He was in the world, and the world was made by him, and the world knew him not" (John 1:10). "Ye adulterers and adulteresses, know ye not that the friendship of the world is enmity with God? whosoever therefore will be a friend of the world is the enemy of God" (James 4:4).

The world seems to understand this, and governments from time to time have made war on Christianity, trying to stamp it from the face of the earth. The pagan emperors Caligula, Claudius, Nero, Trajan, Hadrian, Marcus Aurelius, Commodus, and others with universal power sought to break the back of Christianity, but saints sprang up in those days of the martyrs, so that it could be said, "The blood of the martyrs is the seed of the church."

Polycarp, bishop of Smyrna, was commanded, "Swear by the fortune of Caesar." "Swear, and I will set thee at liberty, reproach Christ," he was cajoled. Polycarp's quiet answer is a classic among martyrs. "Eighty and six years have I served Him. . . . How then can I blaspheme my King and my Saviour?" With that he marched erect to the stake, full of confidence and joy. The fire was kindled, and Polycarp died for the Lord he dearly loved. Thus died thousands of others, but their deaths were not in vain. Out of the bloody soil of Rome sprang the cry of a million martyrs, testifying to the saving power of Jesus. They died knowing that God had not forsaken them and were prepared to acknowledge with their dying breath, "Unresting, unhasting, and silent as light, Nor wanting, nor wasting, thou rulest in might."

The day will come when God will deal with His enemies, as surely as when He delivered Israel at the Red Sea. But how will He do this? In a bygone age when a certain generation had crossed that invisible line separating God's mercy from His wrath, a great Flood lashed the earth, and every living creature perished except those that entered Noah's ark. For more than one hundred years Noah had sounded the message of warning. But men mocked God, derided Noah, His messenger, and, according to the Scriptures, "knew not until the flood came, and took them all away" (Matthew 24:39).

Once again the world faces the retribution that comes with deliberately despising God's grace. When will it happen? What form will it take? The Bible has the answer: "For, behold, the day cometh, that shall burn as an oven; and all the proud, yea, and all that do wickedly, shall be stubble: and the day that cometh shall burn them up, saith the Lord of hosts, that it shall leave them neither root nor branch" (Malachi 4:1). A Negro spiritual says, "God gave Noah the rainbow sign. It won't be water but fire next time." And that is true. "But the day of the Lord will come as a thief in the night; in the which the heavens shall pass away with a great noise,

and the elements shall melt with fervent heat, the earth also and the works that are therein shall be burned up. Seeing then that all these things shall be dissolved, what manner of persons ought ye to be in all holy conversation and godliness, looking for and hasting unto the coming of the day of God, wherein the heavens being on fire shall be dissolved, and the elements shall melt with fervent heat?" (2 Peter 3:10-12).

Yes, God will literally burn this old planet, purifying our earthly home. Man, has discarded hardware in space, where it orbits the earth even as these words are written. He

131

has polluted the atmosphere with the discharge of poisonous gases from internal combustion engines in planes and automobiles. He has polluted the rivers with industrial sewage. Little wonder Peter describes the purification of both the earth and the heavens. The atmosphere that surrounds our planet will burn along with this earth and all man's inventions. The apostle John pictures it thus, "And I saw the dead, small and great, stand before God; and the books were opened: and another book was opened, which is the book of life: and the dead were judged out of those things which were written in the books, according to their works. And the sea gave up the dead which were in it; and death and hell delivered up the dead which were in them: and they were judged every man according to their works. And death and hell were cast into the lake of fire. This is the second death. And whosoever was not found written in the book of life was cast into the lake of fire" (Revelation 20:12-15).

Yes, unfortunately, some people will be destroyed along with the earth because they have loved the world and the things that it contains. They did not disenthrall themselves from the temptations of the enemy. They flirted with evil and courted disaster. They pampered sin as though it were harmless. They will, at last, be disappointed, for their destination is hellfire. "But the fearful, and unbelieving, and the abominable, and murderers, and whoremongers, and sorcerers, and idolaters, and all liars, shall have their part in the lake which burneth with fire and brimstone: which is the second death" (chapter 21:8).

It is interesting that God will ultimately destroy everything man has made and polluted on this planet. "But the heavens and the earth, which are now, by the same word are kept in store, reserved unto fire against the day of judgment and perdition of ungodly men" (2 Peter 3:7).

But the fires of hell will not burn eternally. Malachi 4:1 says that it will "burn them up" and "leave them neither root nor branch." Even in the final destruction of the wicked, God reveals His mercy. He gets it over with. Remember that "the wages of sin is death," not eternal life in hell. It is true that Revelation 20:10 does speak of their torment being "day and night for ever and ever," but this speaks not of the process of their destruction but of the ultimate effect of this punishment. It will be eternal. Nahum 1:9 says that affliction will not rise up the second time. These will be the final hours of rebellion. Man will at last have learned the lesson. He will not try a second time to go his own way, to set up a standard of his own and fight against God.

As we consider the fate of the wicked and this wicked world, we could well remind ourselves that "the Lord is not slack concerning his promise, as some men count slackness; but is longsuffering to us-ward, not willing that any should perish, but that all should come to repentance" (2 Peter 3:9). Let us, then, turn to Christ with all our hearts, and we shall find Him a wonderful Counselor and a mighty God.

Death Come Knocking

Cooling board has come to symbolize the table at the mortician's parlor where the embalmer lays the corpse for examination and embalming. In the traditional use of this term, the Negro has spoken of death. He may refuse to take a certain action on the grounds that he does not want to "end up on his cooling board."

Death holds deep emotional significance to every black man. The funeral traditionally has provided an avenue for the fullest expression of these deep feelings. Bound together by suffering in life, there is the deepest reluctance to acknowledge the inevitable separation that death brings. This accounts for the frequent emotinal outcries that accompany the last services for the deceased. In postslavery days, a band playing mournful music usually led the procession from the church to the graveside, but following the graveside ritual, the band might strike up a hilarious tune symbolizing the "exodus of the soul of the deceased to a happier world."

Negros have been known to travel for miles to "pay their respects" to a departed friend. Traditionally, the minister would do his utmost to reassure the deceased person's next of kin of the dead one's speedy departure to the better world. A funeral, then, normally mingled the expression of joy and sorrow—sorrow for the separation from the immediate presence of a brother, but joy that at long last the deceased had been delivered from earthly struggle. The imagery of our language—the "golden slipper," "long white robes," and "starry crown"—reflects the psychological wounds of deprivation here and the basic desire for excellence which was often postponed to the hereafter.

But what is the truth about death? Is it the "gate to endless joy"? Is it that angel of mercy who spirits the soul into the presence of Jesus? What does the Bible say? "The wages of sin is death; but the gift of God is eternal life through Jesus

Christ our Lord" (Romans 6:23). Death, then, is not a blessing but a curse, not a friend but an enemy. "The last enemy that shall be destroyed is death" (1 Corinthians 15:26). Death is the sentence passed upon the whole human family because of Adam's sin and our own participation in that sin. "Wherefore, as by one man sin entered into the world, and death by sin; and so death passed upon all men, for that all have sinned" (Romans 5:12).

One reason that death is considered an enemy is that it temporarily ends life. When a man dies, he ceases to exist. "And the Lord God formed man of the dust of the ground, and breathed into his nostrils the breath of life; and man became a living soul" (Genesis 2:7).

It would appear from this text that the only thing God put into man was the breath of life, and man, the whole man, became a soul, a living soul. Clearly, then, the soul is not something inserted into man which then escapes to some other land when the man dies. "The soul that sinneth, it shall die" (Ezekiel 18:4). Psalm 146:4 clearly states exactly what happens when a soul dies: "His breath goeth forth, he returneth to his earth; in that very day his thoughts perish." A companion passage to this is Ecclesiastes 9:5, 6: "For the living know that they shall die: but the dead know not any thing, neither have they any more a reward; for the memory of them is forgotten. Also their love, and their hatred, and their envy, is now perished; neither have they any

more a portion for ever in any thing that is done under the sun."

In view of these facts, the following advice is certainly appropriate: "Whatsoever thy hand findeth to do, do it with thy might; for there is no work, nor device, nor knowledge, nor wisdom, in the grave, whither thou goest" (verse 10). We need not worry about any part of the dead coming back to haunt the living. "He shall return no more to his house, neither shall his place know him any more" (Job 7:10).

Of David, Peter said, "For David is not ascended into the heavens: but he saith himself, The Lord said unto my Lord, Sit thou on my right hand" (Acts 2:34). Those who die in the Lord do not go immediately to heaven, but to their graves. Is not this what Job had to say of his own destination? "If I wait, the grave is mine house: I have made my bed in the darkness. I have said to corruption, Thou art my father: to the worm, Thou art my mother, and my sister. . . . They shall go down to the bars of the pit, when our rest together is in the dust" (Job 17:13-16).

But if a man dies, will he live again? "Jesus said unto her, I am the resurrection, and the life: he that believeth in me, though he were dead, yet shall he live" (John 11:25). How can this be? "For we must needs die, and are as water spilt on the ground, which cannot be gathered up again; neither doth God respect any person: yet doth he devise means, that his banished be not expelled from him" (2 Samuel 14:14). Yes, God has a way to resurrect the dead and has declared the time when He will do it. "Marvel not at this: for the hour is

coming, in the which all that are in the graves shall hear his voice, and shall come forth; they that have done good, unto the resurrection of life; and they that have done evil, unto the resurrection of damnation" (John 5:28, 29).

This also clears up another point. If, when a man dies, his soul goes to heaven, there would be no need for a resurrection because the meaningful part of the man would already have gone to its reward. Clearly this cannot be the case. When a man dies, he goes to the grave; but when the Lord returns, He will resurrect the dead. "For the Lord himself shall descend from heaven with a shout, with the voice of the archangel, and with the trump of God: and the dead in Christ shall rise first: then we which are alive and remain shall be caught up together with them in the clouds, to meet the Lord in the air: and so shall we ever be with the Lord. Wherefore comfort one another with these words" (1 Thessalonians 4:16-18).

The dead in Christ will arise at His second coming, and, according to the Scriptures, the resurrection of the wicked will be delayed for a thousand years. "And I saw thrones, and they sat upon them, and judgment was given unto them: and I saw the souls of them that were beheaded for the witness of Jesus, and for the word of God, and which had not worshipped the beast, neither his image, neither had received his mark upon their foreheads, or in their hands; and they lived and reigned with Christ a thousand years. But the rest of the dead lived not again until the thousand years were finished. This is the first resurrection" (Revelation 20:4, 5).

John makes it clear that those seated on these thrones had resisted earthly pressures and had remained true to God's commandments. They are the beneficiaries of the first resurrection. John makes it clear to all that only those who come forth at the second coming of Christ, in the first resurrection, will live and reign with Him. The wicked who have inhabited this planet will remain dead until the thousand years end.

Christ will gloriously change the righteous at His second coming. "Behold, I shew you a mystery; We shall not all sleep, but we shall all be changed, in a moment, in the twinkling of an eye, at the last trump: for the trumpet shall sound, and the dead shall be raised incorruptible, and we shall be changed. For this corruptible must put on incorruption, and this mortal must put on immortality. So when this corruptible shall have put on incorruption, and this mortal shall have put on immortality, then shall be brought to pass the saying that is written, Death is swallowed up in victory. O death, where is thy sting? O grave, where is thy victory?" (1 Corinthians 15:51-55). That is why a Christian does not fear death. He believes with David, "Yea, though I walk through the valley of the shadow of death, I will fear no evil: for thou art with me; thy rod and thy staff they comfort me" (Psalm 23:4).

A few years ago a mother sat in stoic silence while her son and daughter were buried the same day. She displayed no wild outbursts of grief. Only the occasional shaking of her head and the twisting of her handkerchief betrayed the strength of her emotion. When it was all over, for it fell my lot to conduct the funeral service, I approached her and asked, "What is the secret of your calmness?" She replied, "I am sustained by the power of God. My hope is in Him and in His return to this earth, at which time He will wipe away all tears. And there will be no more pain, neither sorrow, nor crying."

Reparations

Recently certain groups have demanded that banks, churches, and the Federal government pay "reparations." It works like this: When any war has devastated an enemy country, the conquering nation, especially America, has borne much of the bill for rehabilitating cities, reactivating industry, restoring the people's health services, and so forth.

In relation to the black man in America, the reparation theory maintains that since for more than 240 years black Americans labored without compensation, during which time great damage occurred to their physical and mental image, and since every institution in America has profited from the exploitation of the black, America owes a great debt to him.

White opponents of the theory point out that it was their great-great-grandfathers who enslaved the Negro and not they themselves. Therefore they bear no responsibility.

The advocates of reparations counter, however, that the children of those who enslaved and exploited them currently enjoy the benefits of that exploitation. They have inherited the fortunes, the farms, and the privileged positions in the government. Hence they exercise power and spend money that would not be theirs had they been left to earn it on their own, or had their great-great-grandfathers honestly labored to accumulate their own goods and powers.

The Federal government has recognized an obligation to the black man, and the Department of Health, Education, and Welfare has for the past twenty years tried to repair much of the damage done to the black race because of slavery. There has been an upgrading of education for Negros. The Supreme Court has thrown open the doors of many advanced educational institutions. The Head Start program aids underprivileged children. VISTA, a type of Peace Corps program, aims at relieving many of the social ills of the ghetto.

In addition, the government sponsors, and private industry participates in, many on-the-job training programs. There is, therefore, evidence that the government is moving to repair some of the damage done to human beings by an unjust and inhumane system.

Furthermore, the churches have long evidenced interest in the black man and his general welfare. Denominationally sponsored black colleges dotted the South long before the Federal government began its efforts in behalf of its black minority. Of all the colleges originally established for black people, most were sponsored by churches. The black man has known for years that when he is hungry, the church will feed him; that when he is naked, the church will clothe him; that when he is homeless, the church will shelter him; and that when he is sick, the church will heal him. In Resurrection City, where thousands of hungry poor from all over the nation demonstrated, in the nation's capital, the fact and effects of poverty and ostracism the National Council of Churches and Seventh-day Adventists ministered to the needs of the people. When, because of civil disorders, the large cities of the nation were largely immobilized and on fire, Catholics, Protestants, and Jews figured prominently in providing essential services.

When the Master established His church, He made it clear that the poor were the church's business. "For I was an hungred, and ye gave me meat: I was thirsty, and ye gave me drink: I was a stranger, and ye took me in: naked, and ye clothed me: I was sick, and ye visited me: I was in prison, and ye came unto me. Then shall the righteous answer him, saying, Lord, when saw we thee an hungred, and fed thee? or thirsty, and gave thee drink? When saw we thee a stranger, and took thee in? or naked, and clothed thee? Or when saw we thee sick, or in prison, and came unto thee? And the King shall answer and say unto them, Verily I say unto you, Inasmuch as ye have done it unto one of the least of these my brethren, ye have done it unto me" (Matthew 25:35-40). An unknown author has written, "I sought my soul, but my soul I could not see; I sought my God, but my God eluded me; I sought my brother, and I found all three."

When will America wake up to the fact that to neglect the ghetto is to endanger the life of the nation? In some of the large ghettos, medical attention is almost unavailable, but disease knows no boundary lines. If proper health measures are not taken in the inner city, the suburbs are not safe. Crime is no respecter of persons. For years the hypocritical would smirk and refer to some condition of crime that existed in some distant portion of the city, far removed from where the speaker lived. But this is no more. We are learning that when the inner city is neglected, the suburbs don't have a chance.

Presently, the subject of drug addiction has come to center stage, but how? For the past ten to fifteen years narcotics have so saturated the ghetto areas of the nation as to constitute a major crisis, but apparently few were concerned as long as this problem was confined to the ghetto. Recently we had the shocking revelation that suburbia has now become the center of narcotic activity and that the young people of the well-to-do and the middle class are now the prime targets of the dope pushers.

There is an interrelationship, and what happens to one definitely affects the other. The wealthy man whose secluded mansion is surrounded by a wall, trimmed with shrubbery, and shaded by trees cannot escape the plight of the

directions now. We are trying to find a big scientist coming in on this train from down in Alabama."

The man was Dr. George Washington Carver, of Tuskegee Institute. He was headed for the House of Representatives to tell of his experimentation with the peanut. When he appeared before the distinguished members of the Senate, someone shouted, "Hurry up, old man." But he did not stop his speech in five minutes. For forty-five minutes he talked softly and reverently of the wonders which God has stored in this humble little plant.

This world-famous scientist was once a slave who had been traded for a racehorse valued at about $300. Moses Carver bought the frail and sickly boy, letting him do light chores around the house. Moses Carver took such an interest in him that he educated the young slave.

Dr. Carver, foremost black scientist of his day, discovered more uses for the peanut than any other man in history and saved the economy of the South through his philosophy of rotating crops. Few men have invested in the poor without receiving in return a bountiful harvest. "He that hath pity upon the poor lendeth unto the Lord" (Proverbs 19:17). Christ in His earthly ministry identified so completely with the poor that He could say, "The foxes have holes, and the birds of the air have nests; but the Son of man hath not where to lay his head" (Matthew 8:20). Christ has motivated thousands of ghetto residents, and because of their love for Him they have come alive with a new desire to discern, earn, and learn. There are no lazy Christians.

poorest inner-city resident. Wall-to-wall policemen are not the solution either. The strong must bear the infirmities of the weak. Even if it were not true that white society enjoys the benefits of an economic base built on slave labor, it would still be true that being the haves would obligate them to work for the welfare of the have-nots. What son of a slaveholder could look upon the effects of slavery on an entire race and sense no obligation whatsoever to undo the damage his grandparents have done?

An elderly gentleman alighted from a train in Washington, D.C., one morning. His form was stooped and his face kind and gentle. Porters rushed up and down the platform peering into this car and that, looking for someone. The old man managed to stop one of them and asked for some help with his bags. "Sorry, pop," he said, "I don't have time to give you any

Equal

When men enslave other men, they must find some justification for it, probably because their conscience bothers them. At times the conscience will trouble the worst offender, for conscience demands a reason from reasonable men. Some men react positively to their consciences, correcting their errors and squaring themselves with the rigid requirements of God's law. Others seek to quiet their consciences by justifying their evil. Such is the history of slavery.

The enslavement of the black man has been widely justified from the pulpit by the theory of Ham's curse. The Biblical story, however, does not justify any of the conclusions many draw from it. "And he [Noah] drank of the wine, and was drunken; and he was uncovered within his tent. And Ham, the father of Canaan, saw the nakedness of his father, and told his two brethren without. And Shem and Japheth took a garment, and laid it upon both their shoulders, and went backward, and covered the naked-

ness of their father; and their faces were backward, and they saw not their father's nakedness. And Noah awoke from his wine, and knew what his younger son had done unto him. And he said, Cursed be Canaan; a servant of servants shall he be unto his brethren" (Genesis 9:21-25).

It is hardly believable that anyone could use these verses to justify the enslavement of a whole continent of people, but some have. First, they allege that Noah cursed Ham. The story reveals that Noah cursed only one of the sons of Ham, Canaan. Ham's skin turned black. On this conclusion rests the foundation for the enslavement of the black man. The story itself, however, makes no mention of Ham's skin pigmentation nor does it say that Canaan, the one cursed, suffered a change of complexion. Furthermore, the sons of Canaan did not inhabit the continent of Africa. So, the whole theory collapses under its own weight of inaccuracy. The story says nothing about a

Abolitionists such as William Lloyd Garrison and the Beecher family helped end the shame of slavery.

(Above) LIBRARY OF CONGRESS; (below) COURTESY STOWE-DAY FOUNDATION, HARTFORD, CONN.

curse of black skin. The enslaver of mankind is totally without justification, and this clause, "a servant of servants shall he be unto his brethren," has no application whatsoever to the inhabitants of Africa. No one can legitimately use it to justify the ignominious slavery that has blighted American history.

The Christian church has not benefited from the fact that most of the slave traders came from so-called Christian countries and that the pulpits of Christian churches justified the slave master and the pacification of the slave. The slave was taught that it was his Christian duty to submit to slavery and to trust some vague evolutionary process to ultimately deliver him from his miserable estate. He was taught that Christ required him to meekly serve his master and contentedly accept his lot in life as inevitable, whereas the slave master was dealing with an accursed people. Even George Whitefield taught this. During the 240 years of American slavery, Southern ministers were remarkably silent about the inhumanity of the slave system itself. Today anti-God militants are using this in an effort to defame the entire Christian church and write it off as a supporter of the slave system. They ignore, however, the historical fact that Northern ministers made the strongest case against slavery and that Christian statesmen took up the cry and would not be silenced until they saw this dread system wiped from the American continent. People such as William Lloyd Garrison, Henry Ward Beecher, Theodore Parker, Ellen G. White, and hundreds of Quakers aroused the conscience of America.

But the root of slavery lies in certain incorrect beliefs of individual human hearts. "Belief in the biological inequality and the racial inferiority of the Negro not only sustained slavery and colonization, but also determined the attitude of the public, the zeal of law-enforcement officials, the reasoning of judicial bodies, the efficiency of administration functionaries, and the definition of policies by legislatures and Congress in all matters pertaining to Negroes and abolitionists. Slavery was not the source of the philosophy. It merely enshrined it, prevented a practical demonstration of its falsity, and filled public offices and the councils of religious, educational, and political institutions with men reared in its atmosphere. So long as the temple stood, men clung to the faith."—Dumond, *Antislavery*, p. 52.

Scientists long ago exploded the theory of natural racial superiority or inferiority, but it did not cease when, in the Civil War, the temple of slavery was torn down. The hope of the world is in the glorious gospel of the Lord Jesus Christ, which teaches the basic equality of all men by creation and their total worth to God as His supreme act of redemption has exemplified.

Many have mounted the merry-go-round of death and don't know where or how to get off.

The Incubator

"Your bag" refers to your method of staying alive and earning a living. Your bag is what you do to get ahead. A doctor's bag is thus referred to as a "medicine bag." There are good bags and bad ones. Some men gamble, peddle narcotics or alcoholic beverages, and rob to stay alive and get ahead. But these are bad bags.

By the way, what is your bag? In many parts of our nation there is a disturbing sign. Men seem to have lost all purpose for living. Multiplied thousands merely exist. They become creatures of the moment, living for the next white weed, or the next shot of drugs, or the next drink of alcohol. They have mounted the merry-go-round of death and don't know where or how to get off. Indeed, they don't know why they should. Thousands live purposeless lives. All the challenge is gone out of this world for them, and theirs is an existence of boring sameness.

The other day I boarded an airliner headed from coast to coast in

North America. Shortly after we were aloft, the stewardesses began serving alcoholic beverages. As I saw many of the passengers drinking, the question occurred to me, Why? Can't these people sit still for five hours without needing a bracer? Are their lives so dull that their nerves can't stand the suspense of travel? Yes, for many life has become one grand bore. Many have centered their affections on material things, only to find that with their acquisition, there does not come the anticipated happiness. Yes, it is possible to live in a penthouse, drive an expensive automobile, and wear the most fashionable clothing, yet be so miserable that you contemplate taking your own life.

On the other hand, the industrial revolution has bypassed others, and they are locked in a cycle of poverty that only those who have experienced it can comprehend. They are just as effectively in jail as if they were behind bars. And those on the outside understand little of the pressures upon the poor or their reaction to those pressures. A dangerous gap of understanding exists between the haves and the have-nots, and America has precious little time to bridge that gap. It would seem, then, that man must be strongly motivated, be he rich or poor, else he will lose his will to live.

The Bible, however, supplies the only answer to man's deepest needs. Left to ourselves, we shall likely set wrong or limited goals, and when we attain them, we shall feel as miserable and as unfulfilled as before. The Bible speaks of unselfishness based on love. Jesus Christ's life for the whole human family provides our highest conception of love. "For God so loved the world, that he gave his only begotten Son, that whosoever believeth in him should not perish, but have everlasting life" (John 3:16). This is the purest expression of love known, for we do not deserve it. But God has conferred it upon us. This is what we call grace.

It is remarkable what happens inside people who have been saved by the grace of Christ. Suddenly they have a will to live. The strongest motive available to man—the love of God—resides in their hearts. They clean up the premises where they live. They suddenly take an interest in their fellowmen and seek to supply their needs. They begin to move upward on the economic ladder. Suddenly they develop a passion for knowledge and a desire to worship God. Though faced with the same environmental circumstances, they now see a reason for living. They begin to attack the shackles that have bound them and to break the bands that imprison others. Their eyes sparkle. They have a spring in their step and a new light in their smile. You know that here are supremely happy men, men delighted with the sheer joy of being alive. The love motive is the key to their renaissance.

Love is the only creative force in the universe. By the force of divine love Christ raised Lazarus from the dead. Love is God's creative power, His character. It is the incubator in which the whole universe was born, for the universe and all that is in it expresses God's character of love. Love, therefore, is the key to our own re-creation. Love provides

"Are our lives so dull that we can't stand the suspense of travel?" © LARRY MULVEHILL, PHOTO

RESEARCHERS

hope for the despondent, faith for the fearful, happiness for the miserable, and life for the suicidal. Love heals mental miseries, reforms the delinquent, disciplines the careless, and lifts up the downtrodden. We must seek love at its source, namely, the great heart of God. For man there is but one approach to God—the avenue of prayer.

Genuine prayer springs from the heart of a man who understands his deep need. This understanding is called repentance. It is a change of attitude toward one's own sinful condition and a basic desire for a better life.

Mr. Spurgeon relates that he thought it a strange thing when he saw the motto "God is love" on a country weathercock. He asked his friend if he meant to imply that God's love is as fickle as the wind. "No," replied the friend. "This is what I mean. Whichever way the wind blows, God is love." Through the cold north wind and the biting east wind God still loves just as much as when the warm genial breezes refresh our fields and flocks. God is love both in severity and in goodness. Whatever be the divine aspect, his nature is love. And divine love requires a response. Indeed, it produces in the heart of the believer the responses required. So whatever your profession, if it is seasoned with the flavor of divine love, you will find life meaningful, exciting, challenging, and worth living.

It is also important that early in life one establish a definite goal for himself. This is true in the choice of a profession. One should work at that which affords him the greatest personal satisfaction. Any occupation can become miserable if one's heart is not in his work. If the profession chosen provides a service for humanity and produces genuine satisfaction, then most likely one has correctly chosen his profession. We should also set educational goals. Many young people drop out of school early in pursuit of fame and fortune, only to learn that the kind of world in which we live places a high premium on academic achievement.

There is available today to the eager and the aspiring a marvelous opportunity for on-the-job training even if the academic qualifications were not attained. Some agencies will pay while you learn. So the door of opportunity is open, and we do have the privilege of improving ourselves if we will. Let us, therefore, set a goal for ourselves in terms of serving mankind, knowing that in so doing we also serve ourselves. It is an inexorable law of nature: "Be not deceived; God is not mocked: for whatsoever a man soweth, that shall he also reap" (Galatians 6:7).

We should also set a spiritual goal for ourselves. Christ is the one example worth emulating, because He is the altogether perfect one. He is the very goal of our existence as well as the source of our inspiration and the energizer of our efforts. We must keep Him in view, for "by beholding we become changed." It is not by accident that husband and wife after living together for many years are often mistaken for brother and sister. The very familiarity in their association breeds similarity. Unknown to themselves, each becomes in many respects like the other.

Have you gazed out over the vast sea of human need and contemplated the responsibility of man to God for his fellowman? We have found the answer to Cain's question, "Am I my brother's keeper?" And in that answer lies the secret of our own happiness and the key to our own need. God is indeed our Father, and we are, therefore, akin to all His children. In the discharge of our twofold responsibility of service to God and to our fellowman lies our only bag that will guarantee us happiness.

Scriptural Index

Art and Photo Credits